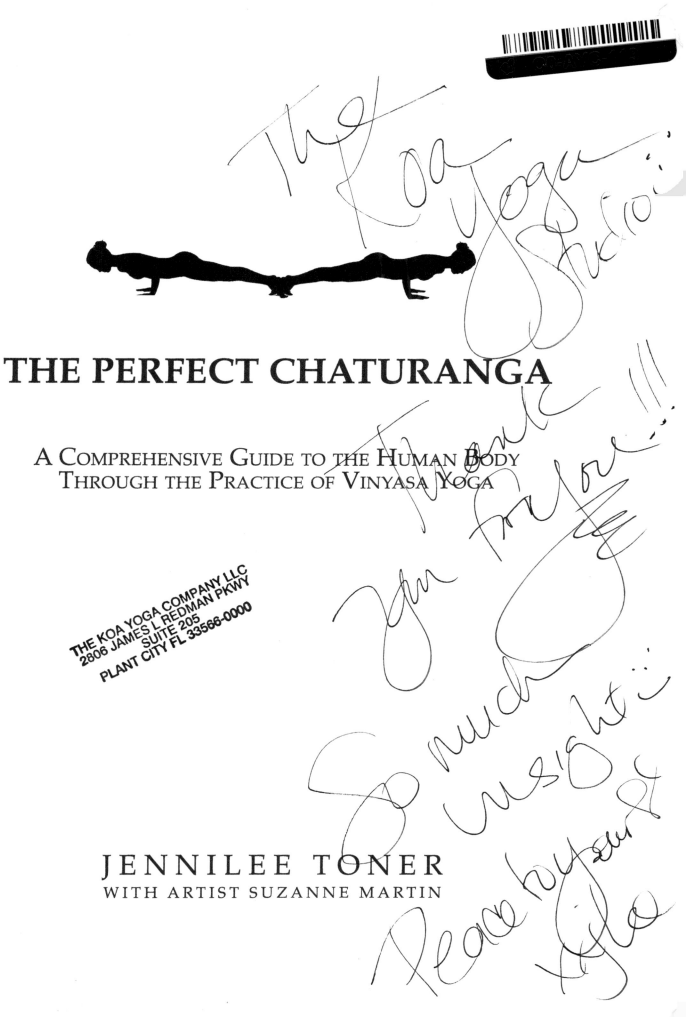

THE PERFECT CHATURANGA

A COMPREHENSIVE GUIDE TO THE HUMAN BODY
THROUGH THE PRACTICE OF VINYASA YOGA

JENNILEE TONER
WITH ARTIST SUZANNE MARTIN

Printed in the United States of America.
First printing: 2014
ISBN: 9781631923739

Attention: Disclaimer
Always consult with and obtain approval from your physician before practicing yoga
or any other physical fitness exercise program. The author, illustrator and publisher
disclaim any responsibility and assume no responsibility for any injuries that may occur
as a result of practicing yoga or any other physical fitness exercise program.
Always practice yoga under the guidance of a qualified yoga instructor.

www.theperfectchaturanga.com

"*Yoga is perfection in action.*"

— *The Bhagavad Gita*

Jai Ganesha, Jai Ganesha, Jai Ganesha Pahimam
Sri Ganesha, Sri Ganesha, Sri Ganesha Rakshamam

Thank you Sri Ganesha for removing obstacles from our paths.
Thank you for giving us the strength and courage
to face and overcome the obstacles you do put in front of us
for the ultimate purpose of learning, accepting and evolving.
Thank you for your grace and your blessings.

CONTENTS

FOREWORD

The Perfect Chaturanga is a book of living art in this ever-evolving yoga world! It is an essential, on-demand tool for all Vinyasa Yoga teachers and dedicated practitioners. Found within its pages is an illustration of a global perspective: wise practical alignment-based yoga can safely lead us to excellent health, longevity of practice, and a tremendous amount of fun!

This work is a collection of Jennilee Toner's yogic knowledge through years of study and practice which has been embodied into her life and consolidated into this treasure-chest that you now have the grace to absorb and benefit from. Jennilee cultivates a variety of themes in her practice and teachings, mainly of self-awareness and of longevity. She is a vibrant woman fervent about the practice of safe and intelligent yoga. I firmly believe that Jennilee is on the leading edge in bringing this information to the masses.

I have known Jennilee both professionally and personally for many years, and I have been blessed to co-teach with her internationally. As we travel the world sharing the beauty and wisdom of yoga, we have witnessed and seen the effects of the other side of unintelligent practice habits. Burn-out, injury and practice abandonment are a few examples. Time and time again Jennilee and I have brainstormed on these and other yoga practice dilemmas. We both agree wholeheartedly that it is through sharing safe and intelligent yoga practices that we can best support our community and affect positive change.

Jennilee's passion, dedication, enthusiasm, and desire to share this knowledge is for the betterment of all Vinyasa Yoga practitioners. I have seen firsthand the benefits of her teaching and methodologies. Now, it is up to you to utilize this information: to study, to practice, to assimilate, and if you are in the seat of the teacher to share its benefits with others. It is with these aspirations in mind that I offer my fullest support to Jennilee for her endeavor to bring this collected brilliance to the forefront of Vinyasa Yoga. I firmly believe this great work will positively influence and ripple out into the present-day practice of yoga!

Namaste ~ Jennifer Yarro

PREFACE

It is so very exciting…this YOGA REVOLUTION! On a daily basis more and more people, in search of health, vitality and inner peace, are rolling out colorful runways of thin rubber-like material to practice *asanas* (physical yoga postures) in order to align and balance their bodies, minds and spirits. Practices that link *asanas* together with breath in fun and challenging *vinyasa* flow sequences have become the commonly taught yoga class in yoga studios, dance and movement centers, gyms, parks, as well as in the workplace. Flowing with breath from *Chaturanga Dandasana* (Low Plank) to *Urdhva Mukha Svanasana* (Upward-Facing Dog) to *Adho Mukha Svanasana* (Downward-Facing Dog) is a pleasurable and satisfactory way to cleanse the physical and energetic palettes after many challenging standing and seated postures.

Unfortunately, due to lack of thorough and proper instruction, improper techniques and common misalignments, cases of joint injuries directly linked to the repetitive motion of these three poses in a vinyasa flow yoga practice are on the rise. Tendonitis (inflammation of muscle attachments to bone), bursitis (inflammation of strategically placed fluid-like sacs in the body) or arthritis (inflammation in joints) in practitioner's shoulders, elbows and wrists, as well as injuries in the spine, are preventing people from coming to the mat to practice their yoga, and attaining the immense physiological, psychological, and spiritual benefits that yoga has been proven to offer.

In order for this yoga revolution to succeed, and for the cultivation and expansion of peace, love, happiness and radiantly great health to continue, proper alignment of these three poses must be practiced and taught!

AUTHOR'S NOTE

What began as a mission to spread the practice of safe and intelligent vinyasa flow yoga has evolved into an extraordinary quest of my heart. I initially thought *The Perfect Chaturanga* would be a simple yoga anatomy and injury prevention book but realized early on that there was so much more to share. From personal experience I have found that the study of the various branches of classical yoga and the practice of modern day hatha-vinyasa yoga can realistically and completely change a human life. The science, philosophy and practice of yoga encouraged me to ask the big questions: Who am I? Why am I here? What are my habitual patterns? How do I relate to the world around me? How does this amazing vehicle of mine, this perfectly working organism, this radiantly healthy, fabulously strong and supple body actually work? What is my *dharma* (my purpose) as I travel forth? This Self-inquiry that yoga inspired and required of me (and actually continues, even at this very moment, to *demand* of me) has enabled me to transform and heal in incredibly profound and deep ways. I am honored to share with you all the riches that I have experienced on my yogic journey. I thank you for letting me serve you. Namaste.

Honor who you are and
where you are on your path,
Know that where you are is exactly
where you are supposed to be!

OM SHANTI
PEACE

YOGA

अथ योगानुशासनम्

Atha Yoga Anushasanam

Now, after having tried everything else, the study and practice of Yoga begins.

-Yoga Sutra 1.1

YOGA

The word yoga, योग comes from the Sanskrit root *yuj*, which means "to yoke", "to join" or "union". Earliest archaeological evidence of Yoga's existence can be found in 5,000 year old Indus Valley stone seals that depict human figures in yoga poses. It is said that in order to know the answers to life's deepest and most profound questions, ancient yogis, sages and rishis would withdraw from all they knew, retreat to nature's forests and mountain caves, and sit in solitude in order to know their Truest Selves. Ancient texts describe yoga as a scientific system of body, mind and spirit integration and harmonization. Most modern day practitioners practice hatha yoga: a discipline of uniting opposite energies (masculine/feminine, hot/cold, active/passive) in both the body and the mind. Unbeknownst to many, the ultimate goal of this system is the merging and dissipating of one's own individual consciousness (*Atman*) with the vast universal consciousness (*Brahman*). In the *Chandogya Upanishad* it is written *Tat Tvam Asi*: Thou art That. Such a simple yet profound truth: I am You, You are Me, We are One.

Ancient Hindu Scriptures

Vedas: Ancient sacred scriptures containing the oldest teachings of yoga: Eternal Knowledge.

Upanishads: Conclusion of the Vedas. Describe relationship between Brahman (ultimate reality) and Atman (individual inner self/soul).

Puranas: Folktales explaining the teachings of the Vedas and Upanishads.

The Bhagavad Gita: The Lord's Song. In the epic poem of India, The Mahabharata, Lord Krishna teaches the magnificent warrior Arjuna Jnana Yoga (yoga of self-study), Bhakti Yoga (yoga of love and devotion) and Karma Yoga (yoga of selfless service).

Yoga Sutra of Patanjali: Foundational text of Yoga. Ashtanga, detailed 8 limbs, is a systematic discipline, practice and path to enlightenment.

Hatha Yoga Pradipika: Oldest surviving text on Hatha Yoga; describes 6 limbs of yoga.

OM, in the castle of Brahman, which is the human body, there lies a small sacred space in the shape of a lotus flower, right next to the heart. Our desire is such that we shall want to find out who dwells here.

If anyone asks, "Who dwells in this small space in the shape of a lotus flower in the castle of Brahman which is the human body? Who is there that we shall want to find and know?"

If asked this we shall answer, "This little sacred space next to the human heart is as vast as the Universe. The heavens and earth are in there. The sun and the moon and all the stars are in there. Fire and lightening and winds are in there. All that is now and All that is not resides in there; For the whole of the Universe lives and dwells in the lotus flower of our heart."

And if anyone should say, "If everything in the Universe is in the castle of Brahman, all beings and all desires, what remains when the castle grows old and the body withers, decays and dies?"

To this we can answer, "The Spirit who dwells in the body never grows old. It never dies. The Spirit who is everlasting can never be killed. In this castle of Brahman dwells all the love of the Universe. It is Atman, Pure Spirit, which is beyond sorrow, beyond old age, and beyond death. It is Atman, pure Spirit, which is beyond evil, beyond hunger, and beyond thirst. It is Atman, Pure Spirit, whose Love is Truth, whose Thoughts are Truth."

-Chandogya Upanishad

Many paths of yoga are available according to the constitution of the practitioner. In the ancient scriptures, the *Vedas*, we are introduced to *Nada Yoga* (Yoga of Sound and Vibration). In the *Bhagavad Gita*, Krishna teaches Arjuna about three paths of yoga: *Bhakti Yoga* (Yoga of Love and Devotion), *Karma Yoga* (Yoga of Selfless Service and Action) and *Jnana Yoga* (Yoga of Study and Self Knowledge). In the *Yoga Sutras*, Patanjali outlines the 8-limbed system of *Raja Yoga* (Yoga of the Mind). *Hatha Yoga* (Yoga of Physical Asanas and Control of Prana) is outlined in three ancient texts: *Hatha Yoga Pradapika, Gheranda Samhita* and *Shiva Samhita*. For every spiritual seeker's constitution there is a perfectly matched path of yoga.

The 6 Branches of Classical Yoga

In the west, we predominantly practice Hatha Yoga, the physical discipline of yoking opposite energies within our bodies. "HA" signifies the Sun, Prana, Masculine, Hot, Dynamic, Yang energies within us and "THA" signifies the Moon, Apana, Feminine, Cold, Receptive, Yin energies within us. Due to the rigors of life and our reactions to the experiences and relationships in it, we often find ourselves askew, thrown out of our natural state of balance. Some days we find ourselves extremely busy and chaotic, other days we barely make it off the couch. Diligent and consistent practice of hatha yoga can effectively work our bodies and minds back into an ideal state of homeostasis, our optimal state of dynamic equilibrium.

The *Yoga Sutras*, written sometime between 200 BCE-200CE, form the theoretical and philosophical basis of *Raja Yoga* and are considered to be the most organized, coherent and complete description of that discipline. In the *Yoga Sutras*, Patanjali prescribes adherence to eight "limbs" (steps) to quiet one's mind. The first two limbs (*yamas and niyamas*) describe a set of moral disciplines and observances to begin easing the agitation of the body and the mind. Practicing the *yamas* (non-violence, truthfulness, non-stealing, moderation and non-greediness) and the *niyamas* (cleanliness, contentment, austerity, self-study and surrender to God) prepares the yogi for the third and fourth limbs, *asanas* (physical postures) and *pranayama* (breath control). The next three: *pratyahara* (sense withdrawal), *dharana* (concentration), and *dhyana* (meditation), train the yogi's mind in order to reach the last limb, *samadhi* (blissful union).

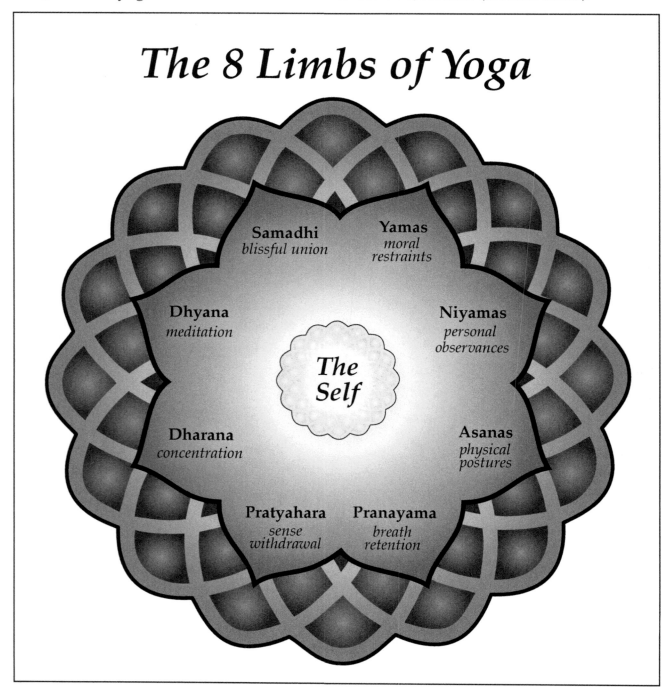

The 8 Limbs of Yoga

Samadhi
blissful union

Yamas
moral restraints

Dhyana
meditation

Niyamas
personal observances

The Self

Dharana
concentration

Asanas
physical postures

Pratyahara
sense withdrawal

Pranayama
breath retention

YAMAS
moral restraints

Ahimsa	non-violence, having compassion for all living things
Satya	truthfulness, communicating honestly & sincerely
Asteya	non-stealing, only taking what is freely given
Brahmacharya	abstinence, moderation of the senses
Aparigraha	greedlessness, not taking more than is needed

NIYAMAS
personal observances

Sauca	purity and cleanliness of body, mind & environment
Santosha	contentment, cultivating happiness with what is
Tapas	passion, zeal, burning desire for Self-realization
Svadyaya	self-study, examining one's habitual patterns
Isvarapranidhana	surrendering to God, recognizing the divine in all

These disciplines and observances of morality and self-restraint become a great vow when applied to all beings everywhere. It is necessary that these disciplines and observances become universal and are not restricted by any means; no matter to whom, in what time, in what space and in what situation. Thank You Sage Patanjali.

Hatha Yoga:
It's Journey from the East

SHIV DAYAL SINGH (1818-1878)
SHABD YOGA

↓

Kirpal Singh (1894–1974)

↓

Walter Baptiste (1918–2001)

↓

Baron Baptiste
POWER YOGA

LAHIRI MAHASAYA (1828–1895)

↓

Sri Yukteshwar (1855 – 1936)

↓

Paramahamsa Yogananda (1893-1952)

↓

Bishnu Ghosh

↓

Bikram Choudhury
BIKRAM YOGA

SWAMI SIVANANADA SARASWATI (1887-1963)

↓   ↓

Swami Satyananda   Swami Vishnu Devananda
(1923-2009)   (1927–1993)
BIHAR YOGA   SIVANANDA YOGA

↓

Sri Yogi Hari
SAMPOORNA YOGA

TIRUMALAI KRISHNAMACHARYA (1888-1989)

BKS Iyengar   Pattabhi Jois   TKV Desikachar   Srivatsa Ramaswami
(1918-2014)   (1915-2009)   (1939-)
IYENGAR YOGA   ASHTANGA YOGA   Indra Devi   VINYASA KRAMA YOGA
                                       (1899-2002)

↓

Gary Krafstow
VINIYOGA

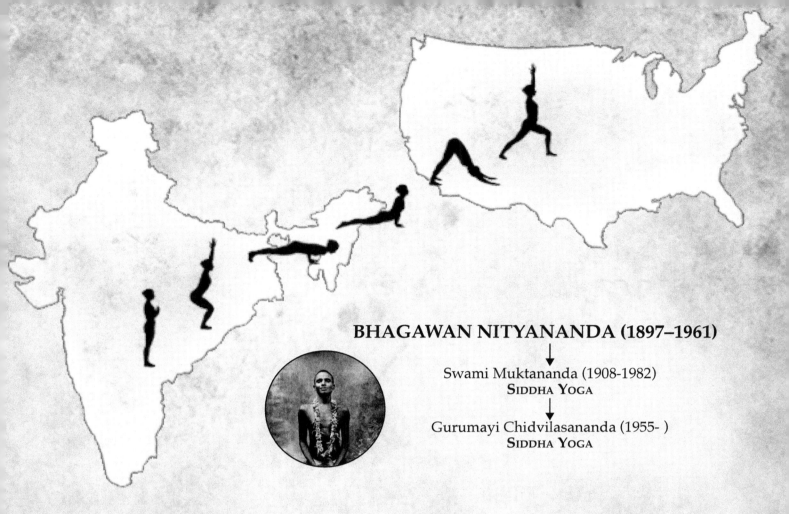

BHAGAWAN NITYANANDA (1897–1961)

Swami Muktananda (1908-1982)
SIDDHA YOGA

Gurumayi Chidvilasananda (1955-)
SIDDHA YOGA

SWAMI RAMA (1925-1996)

Pandit Rajmani Tigunait
HIMALAYAN INSTITUTE

SWAMI KRIPALVANANDA (1913-1981)

Amrit Desai (1932 -)

Kripalu Yoga Center
KRIPALU YOGA

YOGI BHAJAN (1929-2004)
KUNDALINI YOGA

Gurmukh Kaur Khalsa
KUNDALINI YOGA

Vinyasa Yoga

To place the
body in a
certain way
with our breath,
to inspire
movements
and create
shapes with the
subtleties of our
life force energy...

This is Vinyasa
Yoga.

-Jennilee

VINYASA YOGA

VINYASA FOREFATHERS

Vinyasa Yoga, a form of yoga that links *asanas* (physical hatha yoga postures) with movement initiated and continuously supported by breath, has rapidly become the most popular way to practice yoga in the west. Created primarily for young male students in Mysore, India in the mid-to-late 1930's, Vinyasa Yoga's roots can be directly traced back to one man, the father of modern day yoga, Sri Tirumalai Krishnamacharya (1888-1989).

Krishnamacharya immersed himself in the study of the *Vedas* (ancient Hindu Scriptures), first from his father and later in many Hindu Colleges and Universities. After an intense seven year period studying *asanas, pranayama* and Pantanjali's *Yoga Sutras* with his guru in the Himalayas, Krishnamacharya cultivated a dynamic vinyasa yoga practice combining hatha yoga postures, British gymnastics and Indian wrestling. Developed to discipline and strengthen, Krishnamarcharya's set *vinyasa* flow sequences (primary, intermediate and advanced) weave a *Surya Namaskar* (sun salutation) between hatha yoga postures.

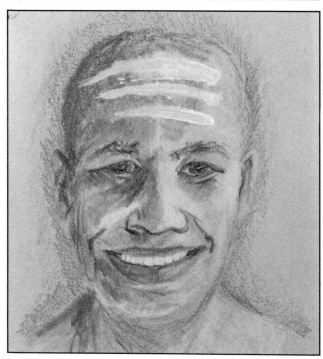

Sri Krishna Pattabhi Jois
(July 26, 1915 – May 18, 2009)

K. Pattabhi Jois (1915-2009), one of Krishnamacharya's students, continued to teach this dynamic vinyasa style of yoga, developing his own system, Ashtanga Vinyasa Yoga, in 1948. Like Krishnamarcharya, Pattabhi Jois prescribed set sequences, from primary to advanced, with emphasis on *ujjayi* (victorious) breath, activating and strengthening *bandhas* (internal locks), and maintaining *drishti* (internal and external focus). After his retirement from the Sanskrit University in 1973, Pattabhi Jois travelled the world to teach his dynamic style of yoga. In 1974, Pattabhi Jois came to America and taught his *Ashtanga Yoga* in Encinitas, CA.

Sri Tirumalai Krishnamacharya
(November 18, 1888 – February 28, 1989)

We bow

to our teachers

in gratitude.

MODERN DAY VINYASA

Building on the trailblazing energy of the early pioneers, western yogis quickly learned the rules of Ashtanga Yoga and then jumped at the chance to explore, challenge, twist and eventually, break them. Although there are many vinyasa flow classes today that continue to pay homage to Krishnamacharya's and Jois' intended sequences, many more barely resemble them at all. In addition to creating new postures and new sequences, modern day yoga classes are made exciting and accessible to all walks of life by offering so many fantastic twists: eclectic mixes of loud dance, pop, rock and world music, lifting weights and using other fitness accessories, hanging from ropes and swings, and balancing on slacklines, paddleboards and other people. The myriad of ways we have taken the tried and true set sequences of our forefathers and infused them with our youthful love of life and play is a testament to how ALIVE this ancient system of yoga still is.

EXAMPLES OF MODERN HATHA-VINYASA FLOW YOGA

Name	Ashtanga	Jivamukti	Power Yoga (Two different schools)	Prana Flow
Style	Vinyasa	Vinyasa/Hatha	Vinyasa	Vinyasa
Creator	Pattabhis Jois	Sharon Gannon & David Life	Beryl Bender Birch Bryan Kest	Shiva Rea
Lineage/ Influences	Krishnamacharya	Pattabhis Jois	Pattabhis Jois	Tantric Bhakti Yoga, Krishnamacharya
What to Expect	-progressive set series -dynamic flow -lots of chaturangas -focus on vinyasa (linking postures with breath) for purifying -focus on drishti (focus point) to stabilize mind -focus on bandhas (internal locks) for breath and mind control	-chanting -scripture -focus of the month -great music -not so many chaturangas -focus on five tenets 1. ahimsa (nonviolence) 2. bhakti (devotion) 3. dhyana (meditation) 4. nada (sound) 5. shastra (scripture study)	Birch: -classical ashtanga -non-dogmatic -non-exclusive -non-injurious Kest: -raw and real language -dynamic ashtanga based flow yoga -attention on personal experience/ personal growth	-energetic -creative -fluid/dancelike -focus on bhava (feeling mind), evolution (waves of vinyasa krama sequences lead to peak flow sequence), integration (intelligent sequencing), energetic alignment & collective flow
Books/ DVDs	-*Yoga Mala: The original Teachings of Ashtanga Yoga* by Sri K. Pattabhi Jois -*Surya Namaskara* by Sri K. Pattabhi Jois	-*Jivamukti Yoga: Practices for Liberating Body and Soul* by Sharon Gannon and David Life -*The Art of Yoga Assists: A Complete Visual & Inspirational Guide to Yoga Asana Assists* by Sharon Gannon and David Life -Jivamukti DVDs	-*Power Yoga and Beyond Power Yoga* by Beryl Bender Birch -BBBirch DVDs -*Bryan Kest Power Yoga Complete Collection* -Bryan Kest DVDs	-*Tending the Heart Fire: Living in Flow with the Pulse of Life* by Shiva Rea Shiva Rea DVDs
Websites	kpjayi.org ashtanga.com	jivamukti.com	Beryl B Birch: power-yoga.com Bryan Kest: poweryoga.com	shivarea.com

***Author's influences. In no way, shape or form is this a complete list of modern hatha-vinyasa yoga.

EXAMPLES OF MODERN HATHA-VINYASA FLOW YOGA

Name	Baron Baptiste	Forrest Yoga	Frog Lotus Yoga	Sampoorna Yoga
Style	Hot Vinyasa	Vinyasa/Hatha	Vinyasa/Hatha	Vinyasa/Hatha
Creator	Walt & Baron Baptiste	Ana T. Forrest	Vidya Jacqueline Heisel	Shri Yogi Harri
Lineage/ Influences	Krishnamacharya, Iyengar, Desikachar	Classical Yoga, Native American Medicine	Ashtanga Yoga , Iyengar Yoga, Forrest Yoga, Kundalini Yoga	Sivananda
What to Expect	-dynamic flow -heated room with added humidity -motivational speaking to empower students -set sequence with room for instructor's creativity -lots of chaturangas -focus on increasing physical vitality and personal power	-fierce, challenging practice both physically and mentally -active hands and feet -focus on doing the work to heal past traumas -focus on Four Pillars: 1. Breath 2. Strength 3. Integrity 4. Spirit	-strong pranayama focus -thorough seated warm-up of all major joints - dynamic alignment based vinyasa flow - intelligent thematic sequencing	-yoga of fullness -dynamic integration of all 6 yoga branches: 1.Hatha 2.Raja 3.Karma 4. Jnana 5. Bhakti 6. Nada Yoga -attention to asana and pranayama -purification and harmonization of all aspects of human personality -you will leave feeling relaxed, refreshed and renewed
Books/ DVDs	-Journey into Power -40 Days to Personal Revolution by Baron Baptiste -Being of Power, -My Daddy is a Bretzel by Baron Baptiste -Baron Baptiste DVDs	-Fierce Medicine: Breakthrough Practices to Heal the Body and Ignite the Spirit by Ana Forrest -Double Yoga by Ganga White & Ana Forrest -Forest Yoga DVDs	-Frog Lotus Teacher Training Manual -Boxed Set: 6 Vinyasa Yoga Themes	-Sampoora Yoga by Yogi Hari -Hatha Yoga Pradipika by Yogi Hari -Learn 108 Ragas Easily by Yogi Hari -Sampoorna Yoga DVDs -Nada Yoga DVDs -Audio CDs
Websites	baronbaptiste.com	forrestyoga.com	froglotusyoga international.com	www.yogihari.com

***Author's influences. In no way, shape or form is this a complete list of modern hatha-vinyasa yoga.

SUN
SALUTATIONS

Om Bhur
Bhuvah Svah
Tat Savitur
Varenyam
Bhargo Devasya
Dhimahi
Dhiyo Yo Nah
Pracodayat

Earth, Air,
and Heaven
May we attain all the
glory of the Sun,
Who will encourage
us and enlighten us
In our thoughts,
words and actions

Gayatri Mantra

SUN SALUTATIONS

"Surya is the Soul of both moving and unmoving things."

-Rig Veda

In Hindu mythology, *Surya,* the sun god, is worshipped as a symbol of radiant health and immortality. Yogis honor the sun and its magnificence with their bodies and their breath by practicing *Surya Namaskar* (Surya= Sun, Nama=to adore, to bow to). Traditionally, sun salutations began as prostrations of gratitude to the east, the direction of the rising sun. The classical *Surya Namaskar* has twelve movements linked by breath, honoring the twelve positions of the sun in the sky from dawn to dusk. Over time, each of the twelve positions has been given a *mantra,* illustrating twelve qualities of the symbolic sun.

12 Mantras for the 12 Aspects of the Sun

Om Mitraya Namah
(The friend of all)

Om Ravaye Namah
(All shining and radiant)

Om Suryaya Namah
(Who dispels the darkness)

Om Bhanave Namah
(The bestower of warmth)

Om Khagaya Namah
(Mover through the sky)

Om Pushne Namah
(The nourisher of all)

Om Hiranyagarbhaya Namah
(The golden source of energy)

Om Marichaye Namah
(The source of rays and vibration)

Om Adityaya Namah
(The son of Aditi – the divine mother)

Om Savitre Namah
(The stimulator and purifier)

Om Arkaya Namah
(The very essence of vitality)

Om Bhaskaraya Namah
(The illuminator of cosmic wisdom)

Classical Surya Namaskar
(variation)

1. (exhale) **samasthiti** - *pose of stillness*

2. (inhale) **urdhva hastasana** - *upward salute*

3. (exhale) **uttanasana** - *standing forward fold*

4. (inhale) **anjaneeyasana** - *pose of devotion*

5. (retain breath) **utthita chaturanga dandasana** - *plank pose*

6. (exhale) **knees-chest-chin pose**
    modern variation: knees down, lie down

7. (inhale) **bujangasana** - *cobra*

8. (exhale) **adho mukha svanasana** - *downward facing dog*

9. (inhale) **anjaneeyasana** - *pose of devotion*

10. (exhale) **uttanasana** - *standing forward fold*

11. (inhale) **urdhva hastasana** - *upward salute*

12. (exhale) **tadasana** - *mountain pose*

सूर्य नमस्कार
sūrya namaskāra

*Modern variation: knees down, lie down

Surya Namaskar
(variation)

1. (exhale) **samasthiti** – *pose of stillness*

2. (inhale) **urdhva hastasana** – *upward salute*

3. (exhale) **uttanasana** – *standing forward fold*

4. (inhale) **ardha uttanasana** – *half forward fold*

5. (exhale) **chaturanga dandasana** – *four legged staff pose*

6. (inhale) **urdhva mukha svanasana** – *upward facing dog*

7. (exhale) **adho mukha svanasana** – *downward facing dog (5 breaths)*

8. (next exhale) **uttanasana** – *standing forward fold*

9. (inhale) **ardha uttanasana** – *half forward fold*

10. (exhale) **uttanasana** – *standing forward fold*

11. (inhale) **urdhva hastasana** – *upward salute*

12. (exhale) **samasthiti** – *pose of stillness*

सूर्य नमस्कार
sūrya namaskāra

Surya Namaskar B
(variation)

1. (exhale) **samasthiti** – *pose of stillness*

2. (inhale) **utkatasana** – *fierce (chair) pose*

3. (exhale) **uttanasana** – *standing forward fold*

4. (inhale) **ardha uttanasana** – *half forward fold*

5. (exhale) **chaturanga dandasana** – *four legged staff pose*

6. (inhale) **urdhva mukha svanasana** – *upward facing dog*

7. (exhale) **adho mukha svanasana** – *downward facing dog*

8. (inhale) **virabhadrasana 1 (right)** – *warrior 1 (exhale chaturanga dandasana, inhale urdhva mukha svanasana, exhale adho mukha svanasana)*

9. (inhale) **virabhadrasana 1 (left)** – *warrior 1 (exhale chaturanga dandasana, inhale urdhva mukha svanasana, exhale adho mukha svanasana, 5 breaths)*

10. (exhale) **uttanasana** – *standing forward fold*

11. (inhale) **utkatasana** – *fierce (chair) pose*

12. (exhale) **samasthiti** – *pose of stillness*

सूर्य नमस्कार
sūrya namaskāra

* This portion of the sequence is performed twice.

THE YOGIC BODY

Om Namah Shivaya Gurave
Satchidananda Murtaya
Nischprapapanchaya
Shantaya
Niralambaya Tejase

*I honor the luminous
teacher within my body.
I am the embodiment of
Truth, Consciousness,
and Bliss.
Peace is always
manifesting within me.
I shine bright in the
splendor of freedom.*

THE YOGIC BODY

According to the yogic view of the physical body we humans are made up of both dense matter and subtle energy. There are five *koshas* (sheaths, layers, bodies): *Annamaya Kosha* (physical/food layer), *Pranamaya Kosha* (life force/breath layer), *Manomaya Kosha* (thought layer), *Vijnanamaya Kosha* (wisdom layer), and *Anandamaya Kosha* (bliss layer). From most gross (*Annamaya Kosha*) to most subtle energy (*Anandamaya Kosha*), the *koshas* expand outward from the body in some theoretical models and, in other models, the layers deepen within. The word *maya* means illusion; even our bliss layer is an illusion. Yogis remind us of this truth: all that we have, see and feel, all of it - a fantastic and theatrical illusion. We are all merely actors on this colorful stage of life; we are all playing our divine parts in this earthy *lila* (play).

Anandamaya Kosha
bliss layer

Vijnanamaya Kosha
wisdom layer

Manomaya Kosha
thought layer

Pranamaya Kosha
life force, breath layer

Annamaya Kosha
physical, food layer

KOSHAS

72,000 *nadis* (energetic channels) course throughout the human body. Wherever these *nadis* intersect is a *chakra* (whirling vortex of energy). There are 3 major *nadis* in the human body: *Shushumna* (central channel of pure state energy), *Ida* (left channel of feminine energy) and *Pingala* (right channel of masculine energy). These three major *nadis* cross seven times resulting in seven major chakras. In Yogic Philosophy, *Shiva* is pure potentiality at the crown of our being and *Shakti Kundalini* is dynamic creative energy said to be coiled dormant at the base of the human spine. Once awakened, *Shakti Kundalini* will rise through each of the seven major *chakras*: *Muladhara* (root chakra, "safety and trust"), *Svadisthana* (sacral chakra, "sensuality and creativity"), *Manipura* (solar plexus chakra, "power"), *Anahata* (heart chakra, "love"), *Vishuddha* (throat chakra, "truth and communication"), *Ajna* (third eye chakra, "intuition") and *Sahasrara* (crown chakra, "connection to the cosmos"). The reunion of *Shiva* and *Shakti* in our own human bodies results in *Samadhi* (a state of blissful union with all that is).

CHAKRAS

SYMBOL	SANSKRIT NAME	NAME/ LOCATION	COLOR	NUMBER OF PETALS	KEY WORDS
	MULADHARA	ROOT CHAKRA	RED	4	SURVIVAL, SAFETY, TRUST
	SVADISTHANA	SACRAL CHAKRA	ORANGE	6	SEXUALITY, SENSUALITY, CREATIVITY
	MANIPURA	SOLAR PLEXUS CHAKRA	YELLOW	10	POWER, WILL, SELF-WORTH
	ANAHATA	HEART CHAKRA	GREEN	12	LOVE, KINDNESS, COMPASSION
	VISHUDDHA	THROAT CHAKRA	BLUE	16	TRUTH IN COMMUNICATION
	AJNA	3RD EYE CHAKRA	INDIGO	2	INTUITION
	SAHASRARA	CROWN CHAKRA	CLEAR/ WHITE/ LUMINOUS LIGHT	1000 (or 972)	CONNECTION TO COSMIC CONSCIOUSNESS

BIJI MANTRA	BODY PART	ENDOCRINE GLAND	SENSE	"I" STATEMENTS	SYMBOL
LAM	FEET, LEGS	ADRENAL MEDULLA	SMELL	I AM SAFE, I AM HEALTHY	
VAM	HIPS, LOWER BELLY, LOWER BACK	REPRODUCTIVE ORGANS	TASTE	I AM CREATIVE, I AM SHAKTI ENERGY EMBODIED	
RAM	MID BELLY, MID BACK	PANCREAS (ISLETS OF LANGERHANS)	SIGHT	I AM STRONG, I AM WORTHY, I AM COMPLETE	
YAM	CHEST, UPPER BACK (THORACIC CAVITY)	THYMUS	TOUCH	I AM LOVE, I GIVE AND RECEIVE LOVE, I AM LOVED	
HAM	THROAT, NECK	THYROID	HEARING	I SPEAK THE TRUTH OF MY HEART, I LISTEN TO THE TRUTH OF OTHERS' HEARTS	
OM	BROW	PINEAL GLAND	PERCEPTION OF LIGHT	I HEAR AND RESPOND TO THE TRUTH OF MY INNER GUIDANCE	
SILENCE	TOP OF HEAD	PITUITARY GLAND	THOUGHT	I AM DIVINE, I AM LIGHT, I AM CONNECTED TO ALL	

The western view of the human body is of anything we can see or touch: Skeletal System (206 bones and approx. 900 ligaments), Musculoskeletal System (approx. 700 muscles and 4,000 tendons), Nervous System (brain, spinal cord and nerves), Circulatory System (heart and vessels transporting blood and oxygen), Respiratory System (organs for intake of oxygen and release of carbon dioxide), Digestive System (organs to process food, absorb nutrients and eliminate waste), Endocrine System (glands and hormones that regulate vital processes), Immune System (defends against disease and infection), Lymphatic System (also defends the body from disease), and Reproductive System. Some of us may have been born with extra or missing parts, some of us may have lost a part along the way, and some of us have parts that are injured, broken or diseased. All things considered, underneath our skin we humans are so very similar. This reflects quite the yogic notion: brothers and sisters, we are the same.

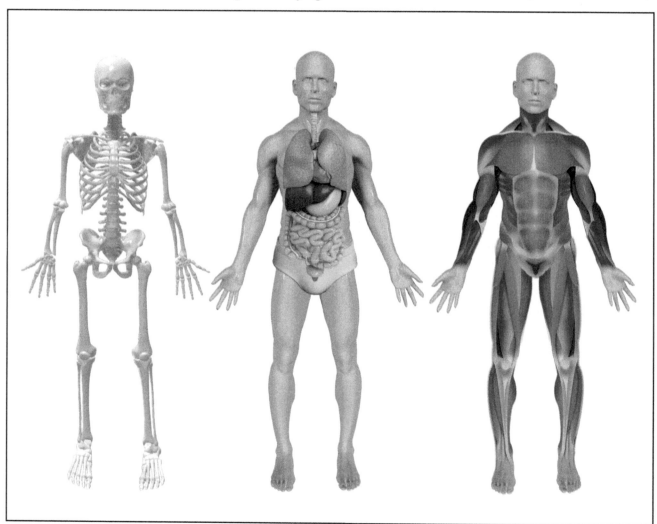

Both Eastern and Western cultures agree that there are immense physiological, psychological and energetic benefits experienced while practicing yoga. Physiologically, flowing from one pose to another via the breath in a vinyasa flow sequence positively affects all the systems of the body. Psychologically, holding *asanas*, listening to the breath and focusing the mind on a *drishti* (fixed focal point) balances and calms the mind. Energetically, people really do feel better, lighter, happier, and more at peace after practicing various forms of hatha/vinyasa yoga.

THE BENEFITS OF YOGA POSTURES

ASANA (Posture)	PHYSIOLOGICAL BENEFITS	PSYCHOLOGICAL BENEFITS	ENERGETIC BENEFITS
Seated	-Strengthens spine -Increases suppleness to hips, groin, knees and ankles -Beginning poses warm up the joints	-Centering -Grounding -Exploring internal environment to get a better sense of Self	-1st Chakra "Land, Root and Connect" -2nd Chakra "Explore, Feel and Open"
Standing	-Strengthens feet, ankles, knees, hips and spine -Tones heart and increases circulation -Tones diaphragm and increases volume in lungs -Cultivates internal heat to purify (sweat)	-Strengthens the ability of the mind to focus in the midst of movement and chaos -Helps clear the mind of old and unnecessary habitual patterns	-1st Chakra "Warrior: Root and Rise" -2nd Chakra "Move and Explore" -3rd Chakra "Agility and Power" -4th Chakra "Peaceful, Open-Hearted and Humble Warrior"
Balancing	-Same as above -Strengthens intrinsic stability muscles -Balances left and right side of body	-Increases the ability of the mind to be light and playful as well as grounded, to be expansive as well as rooted, to move freely with breath, and to anchor in stillness -Encourages overall sense of balance	-1st Chakra "Root to Rise" -2nd Chakra "Move, Play, Be Free" -3rd Chakra "Find and Integrate Your Center" -4th Chakra "Give and Receive Freely from an Open Heart"
Inversions	-Strengthens wrists, arms and shoulders -Strengthens and integrates core -Flushes brain, heart and lungs with freshly oxygenated blood	-Empowering to stand on one's hands -Different perspective on the mat offers a different perspective off the mat -Clear mind of old patterns as you explore new ones	-All Chakras "Root, Rise and Play" "Stable from Your Core" "Pour Heart Energy right down into Mother Earth" "Flushed with an Innate Sense of Clarity and Wisdom"
Back Bending	-Strengthens legs, arms and spine -Strengthens entire back body muscles and stretches entire front body muscles -Stimulates nervous system -Increases efficiency of liver and spleen	-Empowering -Freeing -Encourages the mind to be less serious/more playful ("I used to do this as a kid")	-All Chakras "Root, Rise and Play" "Open Up to All Possibilities" "Shine Bright like a Rainbow" "Kiss Your Belly Button to the Sky" "Close Your Eyes and Go Within"
Forward Bending	-Stretches muscles of the entire back body -Lengthens spine and encourages space between the vertebrae -Relaxes nervous system	-Quieting the chatter of the mind and going within -Encourages introspection	-4th & 5th Chakra "Listen to the Truth being Communicated from Your Heart" -6th Chakra "Listen to and Respond from Your Intuition" -7th Chakra "The Microcosm is a Reflection of the Macrocosm"
Twisting	-Strengthens abdominal and back muscles responsible for rotation -Encourages a healthy spinal range of rotation -Massages and tones abdominal organs -Stimulates the digestve system and helps cleanse the colon -Releases toxins and metabolic waste	-Focusing the mind on the central axis promotes calmness and clarity -Twisting out old patterns and behaviors -Frees the mind to embrace new possibilities	All Chakras: "Regulate and Balance All Chakras as you Twist Out Old, Unnecessary, and Debilitating Energy" "Release Twist and Feel New Life Force Energy Infuse Your Chakras" "Less Dukkha, More Sukkha
Reclining/ Resting	-Cools the body down -Relaxes the nervous system -Aids the body in its quest for homeostasis, an optimal state of dynamic equilibrium (balance)	-Promotes Introspection -Encourages a deep state of calmness, clarity, and peace of mind	-All Chakras "Rest and Allow Rejuvenated Energy to Refresh and Recali brate your Chakras" "Like a Beautiful Lotus Flower, Allow Yourself to Blossom into Your Perfect Wholeness"

Vinyasa yoga INJURIES

Listen to your bodies' wisdom,
Intuit your bodies' needs.

If something doesn't feel good, don't do it.

Always practice with awareness and compassion.

-Jennilee

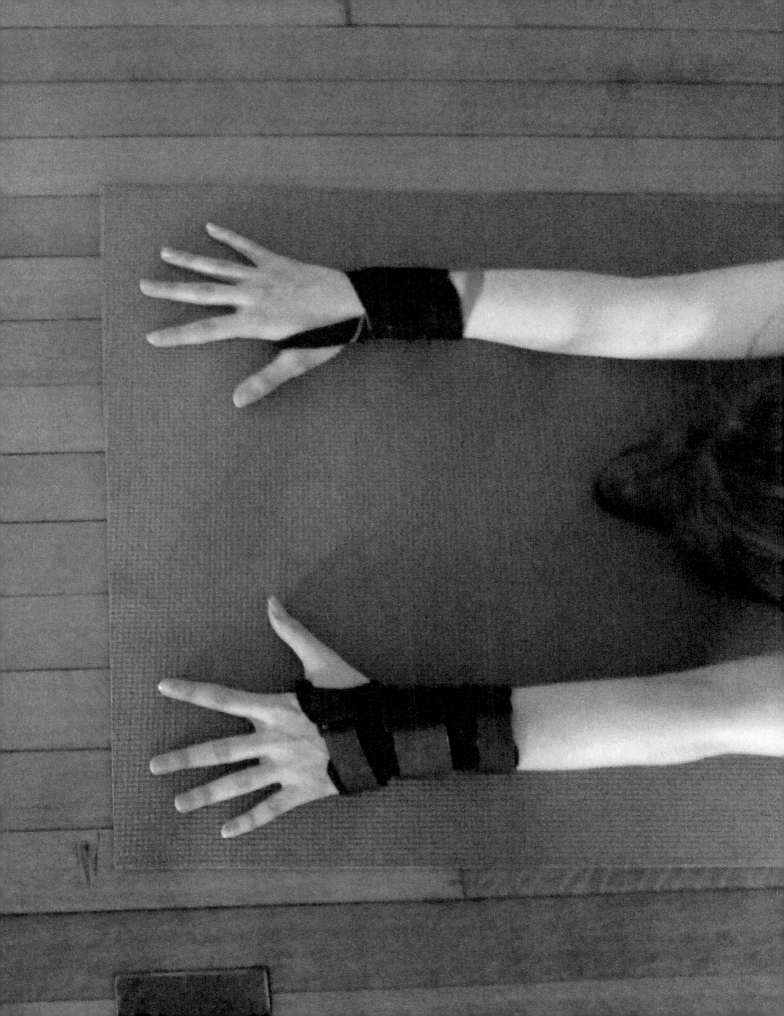

VINYASA YOGA INJURIES

Injury

A wound, trauma, or hurt. This word is usually used to describe some sort of damage inflicted on the body by an external force.

Repetitive Strain Injury

Damage to tendons, nerves, and other soft tissues by the repetition of specific actions/ movements in the physcial body.

Soft Tissue Injury

Damage of muscles, tendons, and ligaments caused by overuse, sprain, strain, or contusion. Pain, swelling, bruising and/or loss of function are characteristics of a soft tissue injury.

In vinyasa flow classes, poses are linked to other poses via the breath. In between standing or seated poses or sequences of standing or seated poses a teacher will encourage a "vinyasa" or a flow of *Chaturanga Dandasana* (low plank), *Urdhva Mukha Svanasana* (upward facing dog) and *Adho Mukha Svanasana* (downward facing dog). Repetitive motion of these three common asanas can lead, unfortunately, to repetitive motion injury, especially in shoulders, elbows and wrists. If a teacher does not skillfully lead a practitioner through this sequence, allowing for self-exploration and modifications, injurious misalignments can be imprinted in the human body. Tendonitis (inflammation of a tendon), bursitis (inflammation of a bursa) and/or arthritis (inflammation of a joint) due to wear and tear are the common vinyasa yoga related injuries.

What is tendonitis?

A tendon is a tough, fibrous cord of connective tissue attaching muscles to bones. Smooth gliding tendons help skeletal muscles move bones via joints. When smooth gliding is impaired due to strain, repetitive motion and/or misalignment, tendons get irritated and inflamed. Tendonitis is the inflammation of a tendon.

What is bursitis?

A bursa is a fluid filled sac that, in a joint, acts as a cushion between muscle and bone. The bursa reduces friction due to movement, helping to keep the joint flexible. Constant pressure, friction and pinching of bursas will lead to irritation and inflammation. Bursitis is the inflammation of a bursa.

What is arthritis?

A joint is where two bones meet. Bones are connected to bones via connective tissue called ligaments. A joint is encased in a synovial sheath and filled with synovial fluid. Damage from trauma, overuse, and/or disease can lead to pain, swelling and stiffness in the joint. Athritis is the inflammation of a joint.

Signs and Symptoms of Common Vinyasa Yoga Injuries

Shoulder/Rotator Cuff/ Upper Bicep Tendon
- pain when moving arm up and down
- pain under pressure
- pain anytime day or night
- tenderness and swelling

Elbow
- pain when extending (straightening)
- pain at night and first thing in the morning
- tenderness and swelling
- burning/hot sensation after activity
- stiffness when trying to bend elbow under pressure

Wrist
- pain while under strain
- pain while moving in any direction
- pain anytime day or night
- tenderness and swelling
- burning /hot sensation
- stiffness/inability to rotate wrist fully

Shoulder Tendonitis
inflammation of the tendon attachment where the muscle connects to the bone

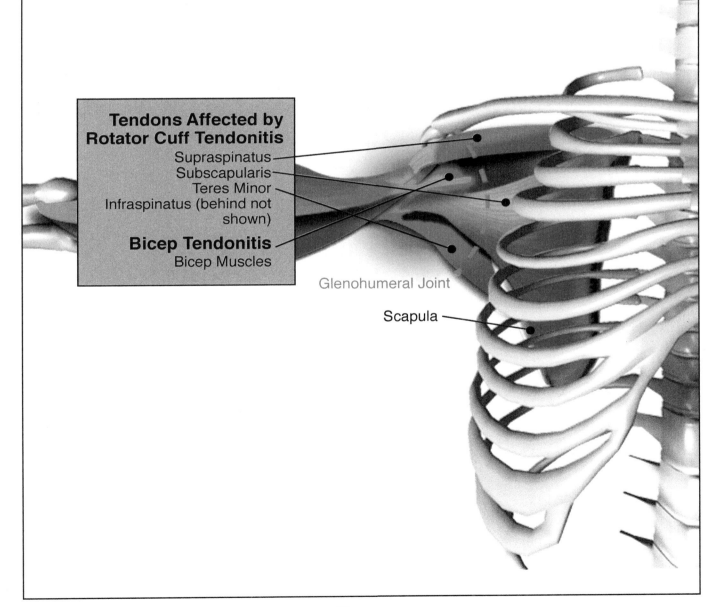

Tendons Affected by Rotator Cuff Tendonitis
Supraspinatus
Subscapularis
Teres Minor
Infraspinatus (behind not shown)

Bicep Tendonitis
Bicep Muscles

Glenohumeral Joint

Scapula

Shoulder Bursitis
inflammation of the synovial filled sac that protects bones from friction

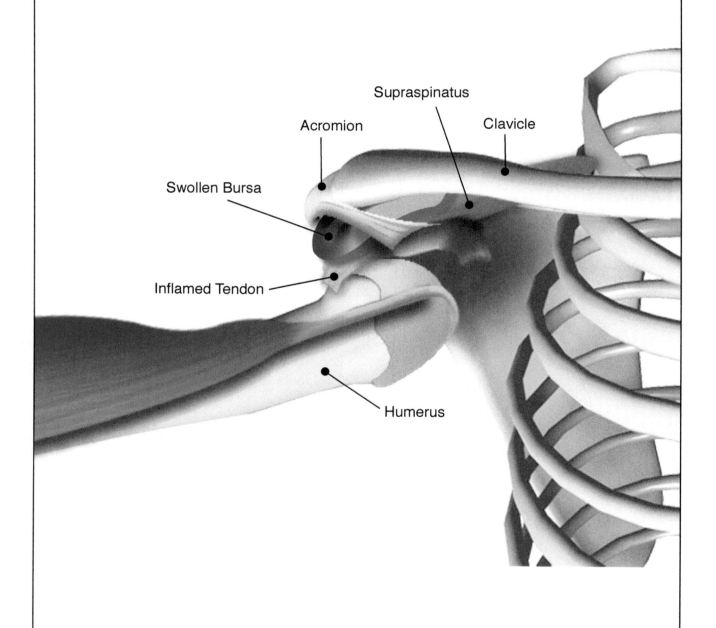

Shoulder Arthritis
inflammation in joints

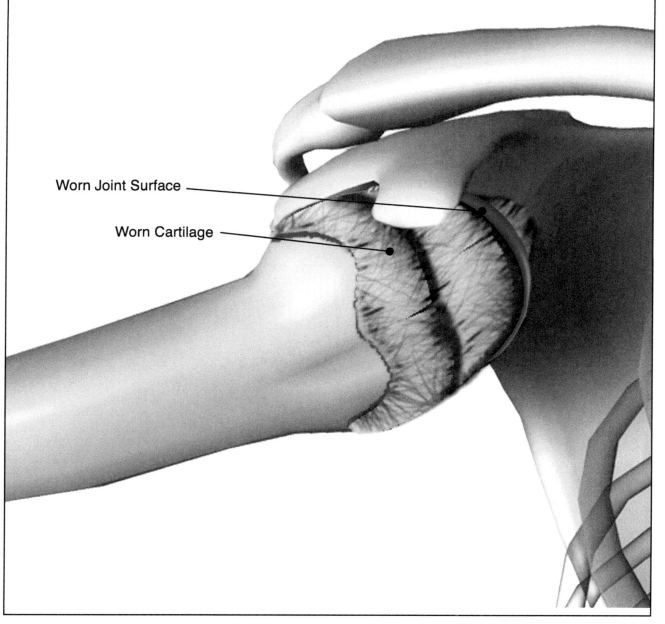

Worn Joint Surface

Worn Cartilage

Elbow Tendonitis
inflammation of the tendons of the elbow

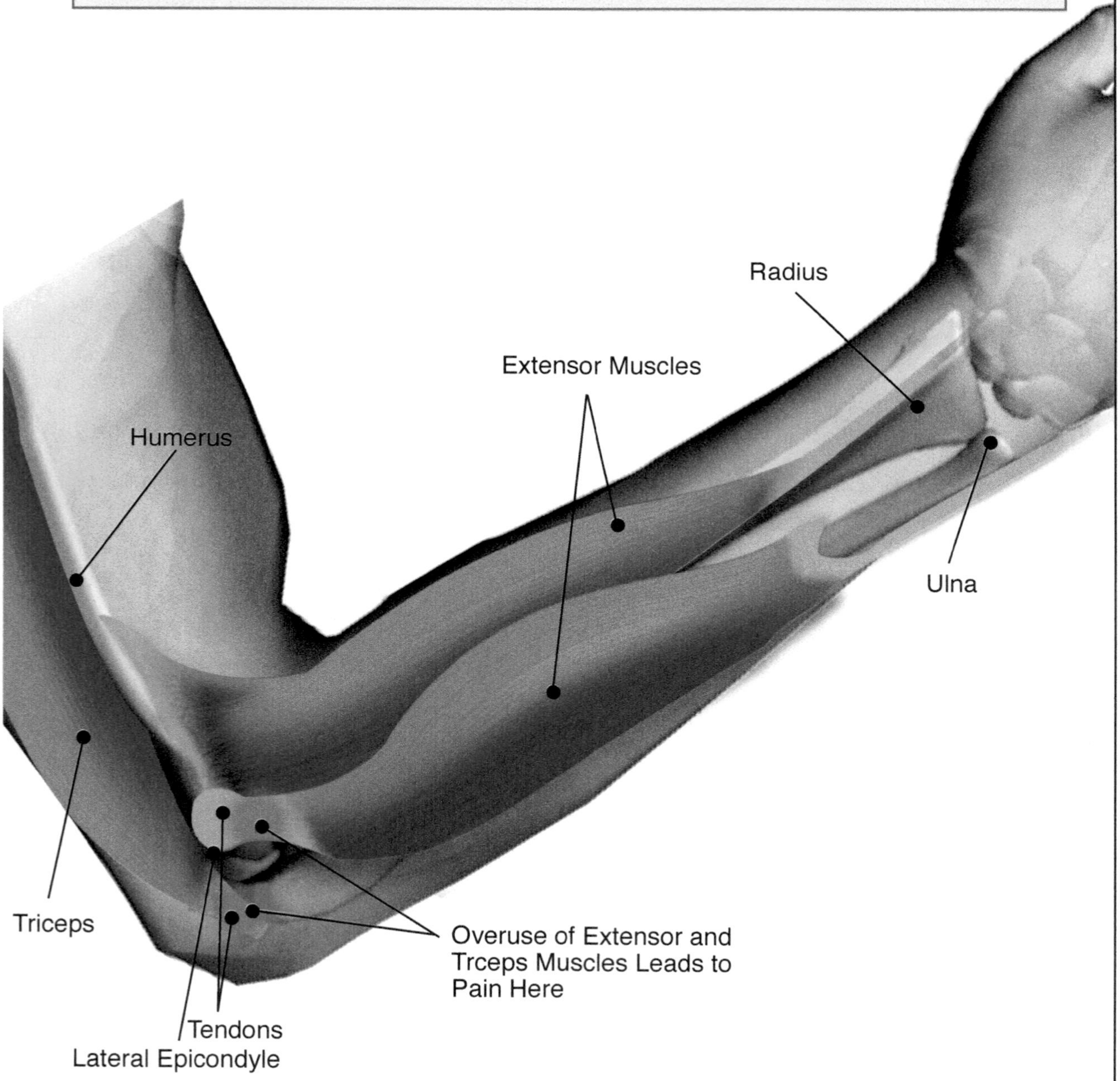

Radius

Extensor Muscles

Humerus

Ulna

Triceps

Overuse of Extensor and
Trceps Muscles Leads to
Pain Here

Tendons

Lateral Epicondyle

Elbow Bursitis
inflammation of the bursa of the elbow

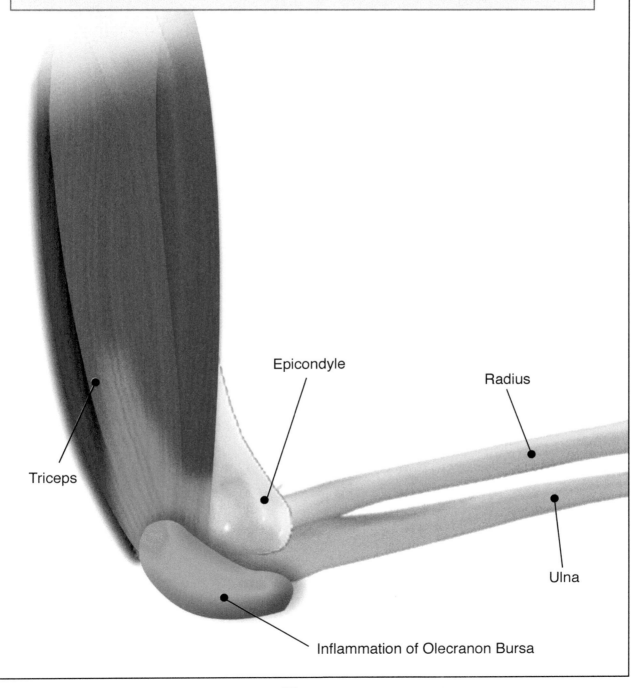

Epicondyle

Radius

Triceps

Ulna

Inflammation of Olecranon Bursa

Wrist Tendonitis
inflammation of the tendons of the wrist

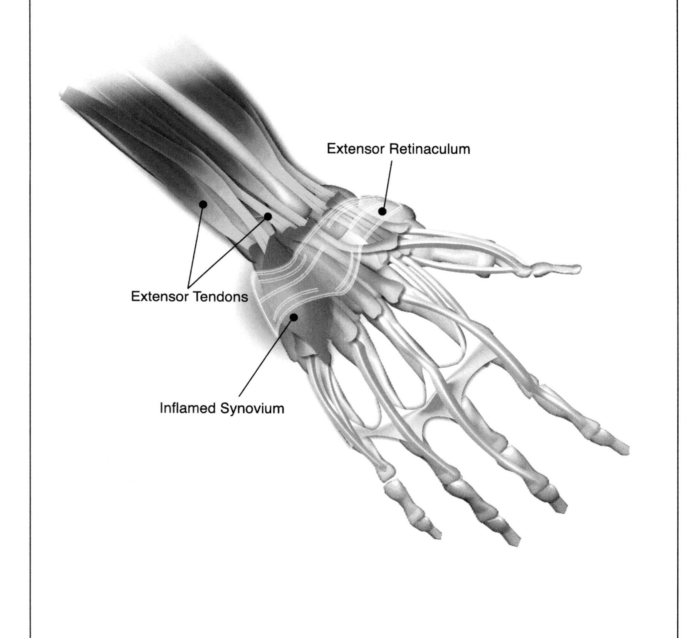

Extensor Retinaculum

Extensor Tendons

Inflamed Synovium

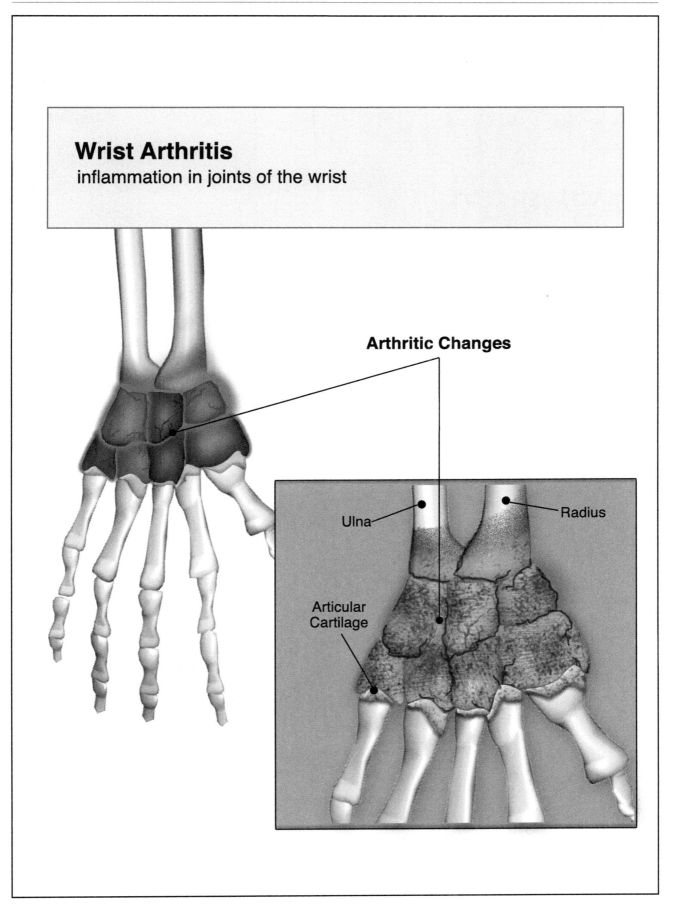

Wrist Arthritis
inflammation in joints of the wrist

Arthritic Changes

Ulna

Radius

Articular
Cartilage

INJURY PREVENTION

स्थिरसुखमासनम्

Sthira-Sukham-Asanam

Practice yoga postures with both strength and ease. This will give rise to harmony within the body.

-Yoga Sutra 46

INJURY PREVENTION

Initial Guidelines for Practicing Safe Yoga

1. Find a knowledgeable (well-trained in yoga & anatomy) and accessible yoga teacher.

2. Choose a class appropriate to your physical fitness level.

3. If brand new to yoga/flow yoga, find a class titled: Yoga Basics, Vinyasa Yoga 101, Introduction to Vinyasa Flow Yoga, etc.

4. ALWAYS listen to the wisdom of your body. Ultimately it is your responsibility to take care of yourself, respecting your physical limitations. If it hurts – DON'T DO IT!

5. Remember, practicing yoga is not a competition! Keep your mind focused on what is happening on your mat, in your body!

According to the U.S. Consumer Product Safety Commission, there were 7,369 yoga-related injuries treated in doctors' offices, clinics, and emergency rooms in 2010 (an increase from 3,700 in 2004 and 5,500 in 2007). The most common yoga injuries are repetitive strain injuries and over-stretching muscles, tendons and ligaments. The initial, most common sense guidelines to preventing injury on the yoga mat is to find a well-trained teacher, an appropriate level class and ALWAYS, ALWAYS listen to your body and respect your physical limitations. Pattabhis Jois is well-known for his reminder, *"Practice and all is coming."* With safe, consistent and diligent practice optimal results will be achieved.

A Safe Vinyasa Flow Class

• Begin by finding and centering on breath.

• Allow ample time to warm up and lubricate your joints.

• Intelligently and safely build the flow of sequences from lower center of gravity to higher.

• Always do at least one cobra (if not 3) before first Upward Facing Dog.

• Allow ample time for slowing down activity and cooling down the systems of the body.

• Cluster your backbends and then do a back stabilizer. No hugging knees to chest or child's pose between backbends! (This compromises the connection between the lumbar spine and sacrum).

• After stabilizing the back, do gentle forward bends before deeper forward bends, hip openers and twists.

• Always finish with a relaxing, supine posture (i.e. savasana, corpse pose).

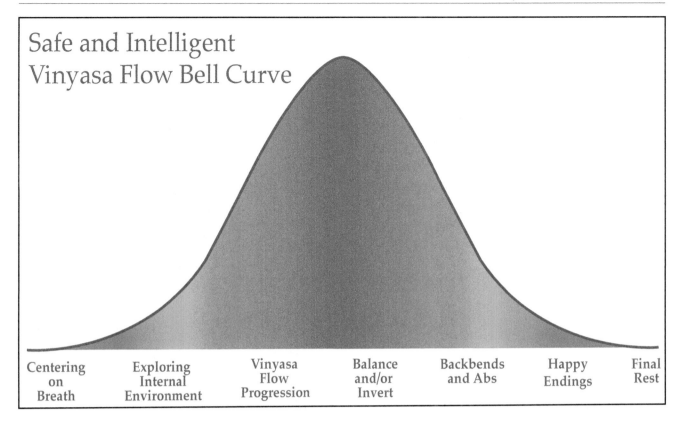

Safe and Intelligent
Vinyasa Flow Bell Curve

| Centering on Breath | Exploring Internal Environment | Vinyasa Flow Progression | Balance and/or Invert | Backbends and Abs | Happy Endings | Final Rest |

CENTERING ON BREATH – Landing in the present moment. All awareness on your breath as you quiet the chatter of the mind.

EXPLORING INTERNAL ENVIRONMENT – Encouraging breath to move and warm up your body. Explore where there is tension, tightness and energetic blockages. Also notice where there is suppleness and freedom.

VINYASA FLOW PROGRESSION –Start with easy, lower center of gravity sequences and then add safe, intelligent and creative levels of difficulty.

BALANCE/INVERT – After Peak Flow pause in stillness. In the midst of all the dynamic movement find your center and balance.

ABS AND BACKBENDS – Keep your *PRANA* flowing but start to cool down. Lower practice to the floor but keep movements dynamic and invigorating.

HAPPY ENDINGS –Everything we eat, drink, think, feel, say, or do leaves a chemical waste in the cells of our body. Hips Openers, Forward Bends and Twists encourage us to go deep within, release and let go of our *DUKKHA*.

FINAL REST – In *Savasana*, relax and focus on deepening and lengthening exhales. Connect to the place within you of profound, eternal peace.

5 STEP PROCESS: BREATH, BANDHAS, ALIGNMENT, ACTIVATION & INTEGRATION

In order to ensure the longevity of your vinyasa yoga practice you will need to learn how to navigate safely, intelligently, efficiently and effectively. Five key ways to do this is to learn how to harness *prana* (life force energy) by allowing movement to be inspired and supported by your breath, activate your *bandhas* (internal locks) for increased physiological and energetic support, properly align your bones in *asanas* (postures) so as not to overstress the connective tissue in and around a joint, and support this alignment with proper muscle activation, joint integration and whole body awareness.

5 Step Process for Vinyasa Flow Practice Longevity

1. BREATH:
Prana is life force energy. We forge an intimate relationship with it by listening to our breath and feeling it course through our body. When completely present, yogis allow breath to both inspire and initiate all movement.

2. BANDHAS:
Internal locks that draw and hold the subtle Shakti energy up into the body. Once experienced, strengthened, and activated, bandhas can and will aid in a yogi's quest for lightness of being.

3. ALIGNMENT:
In order to experience postures in the most efficient, effective and exhilarating way possible we need to align our bones in the way they were meant to be aligned. Bone stacking takes less muscular energy than when we are askew.

4. ACTIVATION:
Certain skeletal muscles do specific primary jobs. Knowing and feeling these muscles will help you move in and out of postures and maintain stillness in postures with ease.

5. INTEGRATION:
To strengthen and protect our joints, especially as we age, we need to be able to align our bones and activate our muscles. In addition, becoming aware of the importance of myofascia, feeling its subtle sensations as it wraps around everything in our bodies (muscles, organs, and the spaces inbetween) helps us in our quest to fully experience the integration of our body as a whole.

PRANA

There are five characteristics of *Prana* (Life Force Energy) that we humans can connect to and emulate: upward, downward, expansive, contractive, and circulatory. If allowed to flow freely without any physiological, psychological or energetic blockages, breath inhaled wants to propel us forward and up; breath exhaled encourages us to come down and draw back. Inhales naturally expand us, and exhales naturally contract us. In stillness we can feel the swirling of energy within our body, our cells, and even, our *nadis* (energetic pathways). Through proper training and diligent practice, a practitioner can harness, and ultimately, direct these five *vayus* (winds). On the mat and off, yogis are floating through life with grace and ease on the waves of *Prana*.

FIVE VAYUS

Prana Vayu: IN
Enters the body via the breath and initiates the processes of all other vayus.

Apana Vayu: DOWN AND OUT
Moves down through the lower abdominal region and controls the processes of elimination.

Udana Vayu: UP
Travels upward through the larynx (vocal chords), trachea (windpipe) and the pharynx (back of mouth/top of throat) and governs vocal sounds. Also, the nourishment of the brain and the inspiration of thought.

Samana Vayu: PERIPHERY TO THE CORE
Stokes and churns the digestive fires and aides in the process of assimilation.

Vyana Vayu: HEART TO THE PERIPHERY
Situated in the heart, governs circulation and movement, and assists the other vayus.

Breath and Prana

inhalation - **puraka**   breath retention - **kumbhaka**   exhalation - **rechaka**

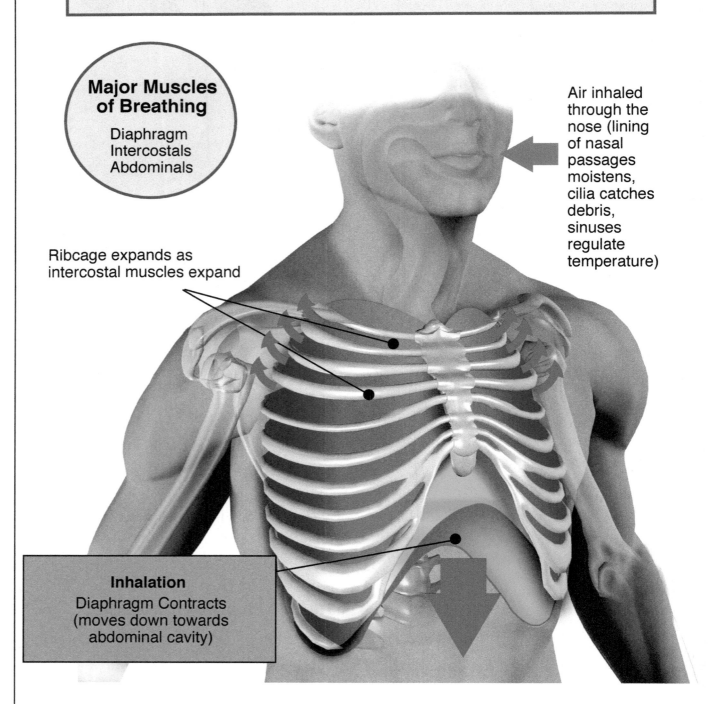

Major Muscles of Breathing

Diaphragm
Intercostals
Abdominals

Air inhaled through the nose (lining of nasal passages moistens, cilia catches debris, sinuses regulate temperature)

Ribcage expands as intercostal muscles expand

Inhalation
Diaphragm Contracts
(moves down towards abdominal cavity)

Ujjayi Pranayama: Victorious Breath

The most common breath practiced in vinyasa yoga is an audible breath known as Ujjayi. By slightly constricting the epiglottis at the back off the throat, the breath enters the body in a long slow stream. This closed mouth breath is often referred to as an oceanic breath or a Darth Vader breath; it is as if you are fogging a mirror on the back of your front teeth. There are many benefits to practicing ujjayi pranayama continuously throughout your vinyasa flow: it deepens and regulates the breath, calms and anchors the mind, warms and helps make supple muscles and joints, heats and helps detoxify the internal environment of the body, energizes and unifies all systems of the body, and helps to create a powerful rhythmic flow of Prana for the body and mind to effortlessly and joyously ride. Over time, advanced yogis will notice that their ujjayi breath becomes more silent, subtle, and internal.

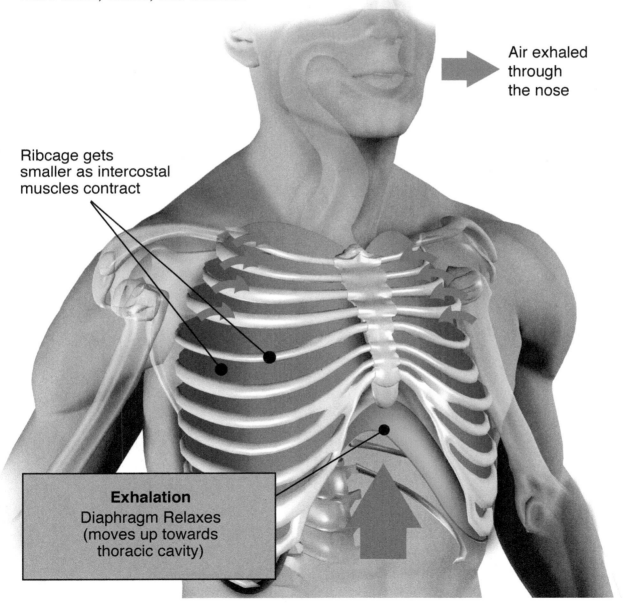

Air exhaled through the nose

Ribcage gets smaller as intercostal muscles contract

Exhalation
Diaphragm Relaxes
(moves up towards thoracic cavity)

BANDHAS

Laws of gravity are such that we are constantly being pulled towards the Earth. Although we are very grateful for gravity (otherwise we would be floating out in space), we yogis do our best to defy gravity and reverse the effects it has on our internal environment. As we age, not only does our skin succumb to the downward pull but also does our innards (organs, tissues, fluids and cells). It is important that we do all that we can to support and tone the muscular system of the pelvis and organs within. Inverting (turning upside down in poses), is one way to reverse the ravages of time. Another is activating our *bandhas* (internal locks) and encouraging a magnificent sense of lightness as we gather and hold *Prana* up into our bodies.

Mula Bandha
root lock

The subtle lifting and toning of the pelvic floor muscles:
- Encourages a tangible lightness of being
- Can be activated during both inhales and exhales
- Sensation: as if drawing a tissue up through the cellophane of a tissue box

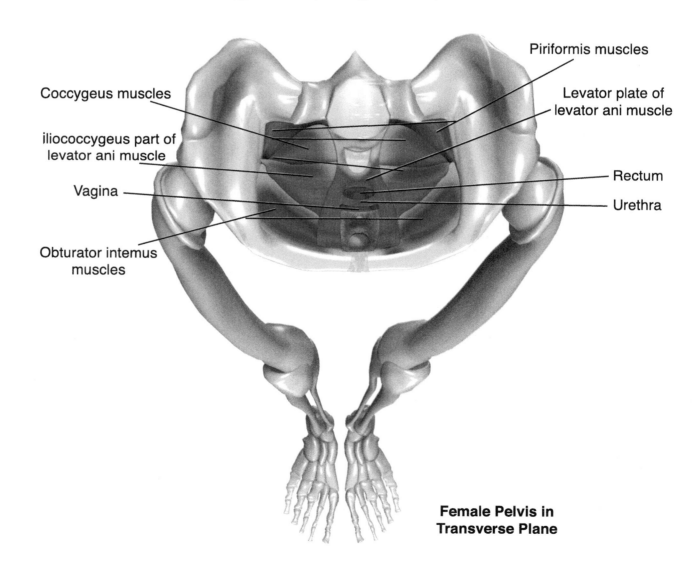

Piriformis muscles

Coccygeus muscles

Levator plate of
levator ani muscle

iliococcygeus part of
levator ani muscle

Rectum

Vagina

Urethra

Obturator intemus
muscles

**Female Pelvis in
Transverse Plane**

Uddiyana Bandha
upward flying lock

• Abdominal muscles drawing navel to spine and up towards ribs

• Tones the diaphragm (major muscle of breathing)

• Activated at the bottom of an exhale, especially when preparing to float in air

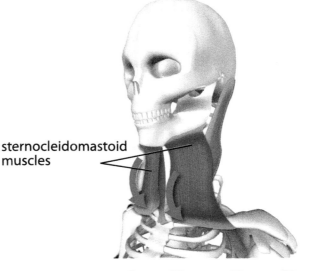

sternocleidomastoid muscles

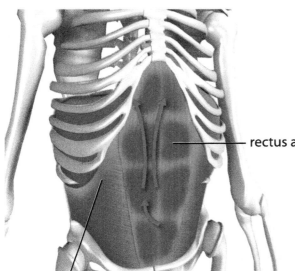

rectus abdominus

transverse abdominus

Jalandhara Bandha
throat lock

• Sternocleidomastoid muscles draw chin down to lifted sternum (chest bone)

• Massages thyroid

• Activated at the bottom of an exhale during pranayama exercises (specific breathwork)

Maha Bandha
the great lock

• All three bandhas activated simultaneously

• At the bottom of the exhale activate Mula, Uddiyana and Jalandhara Bandhas (in that order)

• With diligent and consistent practice, advanced yogis become aware that once one bandha is even subtly engaged, all bandhas will be engaged.

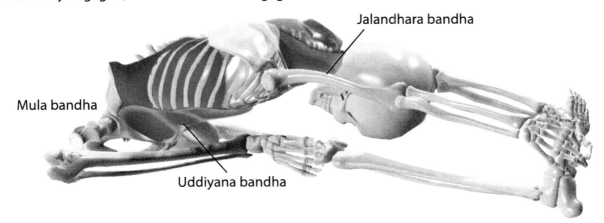

Jalandhara bandha

Mula bandha

Uddiyana bandha

Janu sirsasana (head-to-knee pose)

ALIGNMENT

The skeletal system, in its brilliant design, is meant to stack perfectly as well as move freely into all kinds of positions. There are 206 bones in the human body. Long bones are for levering the body into motion, short bones are for weight bearing, and flat bones are for protection and offer a wider surface area for many muscles to attach to. Where two bones meet is a joint. Bones are connected to bones by ligaments (thick, fibrous bands of connective tissue that are NOT elastic). Muscles are attached to bones by tendons (fibrous bands of connective tissue that are more flexible than ligaments). In the next few pages we will explore how bones stack and how joints move. A thorough illustration of all the major joint movements in the body and the muscles that perform them will follow.

Axial Skeleton
cranium (skull), spinal column, sternum, and rib cage

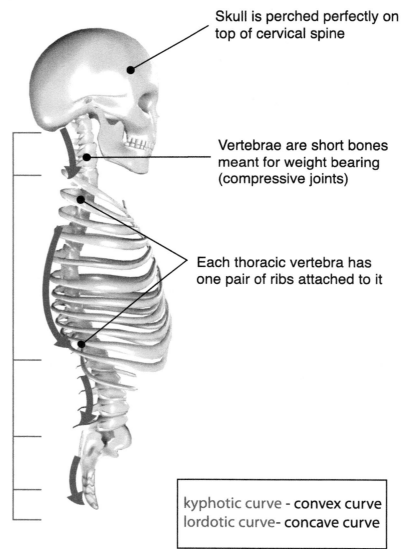

Skull is perched perfectly on top of cervical spine

7 Cervical Vertebrae
cervical lordotic curve
created during infancy
locust and crawling

Vertebrae are short bones meant for weight bearing (compressive joints)

12 Thoracic Vertebrae
kyphotic curve
created in womb

Each thoracic vertebra has one pair of ribs attached to it

5 Lumbar Vertebrae
lumbar lordotic curve
created during standing and walking

5 Fused Sacrum Vertebrae
kyphotic curve
also created in womb

2-4 Coccyx Vertebrae
kyphotic curve
also created in womb

kyphotic curve - convex curve
lordotic curve- concave curve

Appendicular Skeleton
shoulder girdle, pelvic girdle, and their extremities

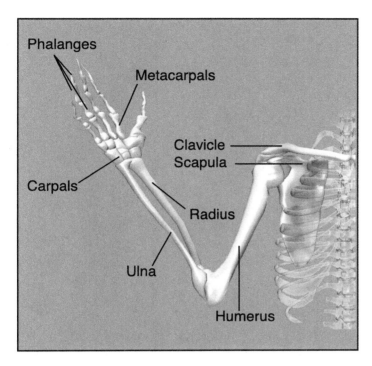

• Shoulder joint is a shallow ball and socket joint comprised of humerus in joint made by clavicle and scapula

• Lots of mobility, less stability (ligaments reflect this by being thin)

• Shoulder joint and arm bones attached to axial skeleton by only one small joint: Sternal-clavicle joint

• Elbow is a hinge joint – only hinges forward and returns to straight!

• Carpal (wrist) bones are weight bearing bones…for some people not since they stopped crawling on them!

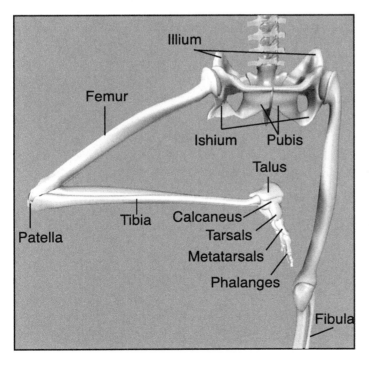

• Hip joint is a deep ball and socket joint comprised of the femur in the acetabulum of the illium, a deep socket that creates lots of stability

• Less natural mobility than shoulder (ligaments reflect this by being thick and wide)

• Hip joint and leg bones are attached to axial skeleton by a big, strong, well-ligamented joint: Sacral-Iliac joint

• Knee is a hinge joint – only hinges backwards and returns to straight!

• Talus (ankle) and Calcaneus (heel) are weight bearing bones... they hold up the rest of body!

BONE STACKING IN POSTURES

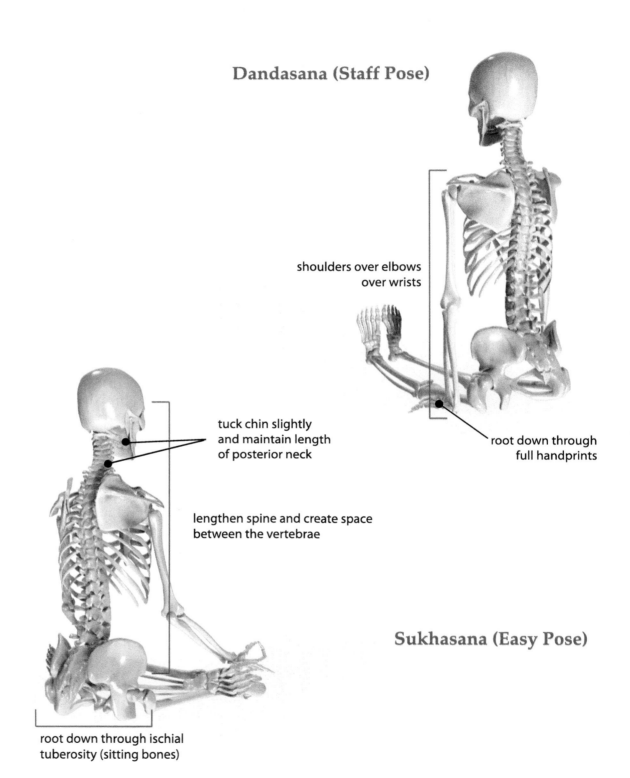

Dandasana (Staff Pose)

shoulders over elbows
over wrists

root down through
full handprints

tuck chin slightly
and maintain length
of posterior neck

lengthen spine and create space
between the vertebrae

Sukhasana (Easy Pose)

root down through ischial
tuberosity (sitting bones)

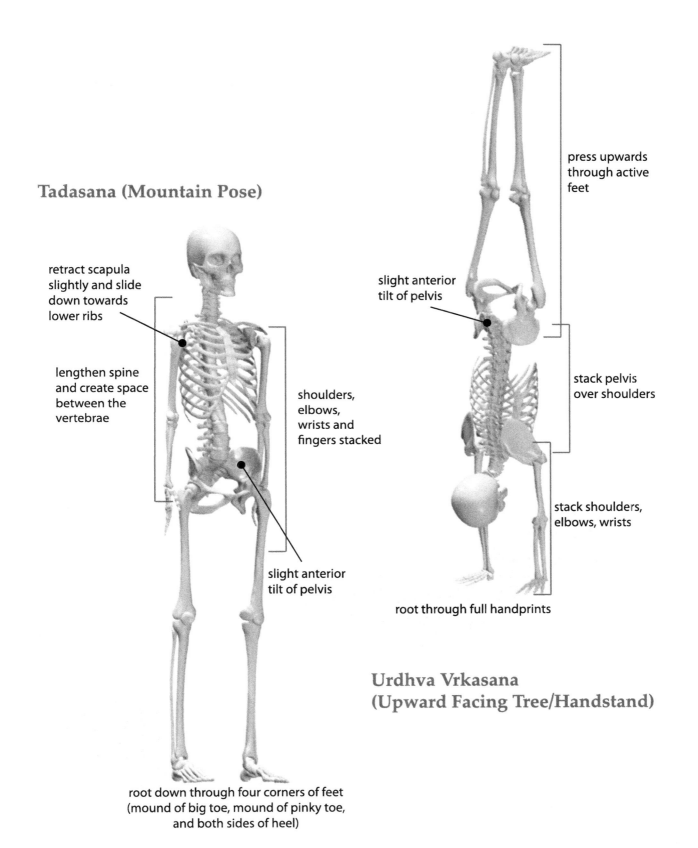

Tadasana (Mountain Pose)

retract scapula slightly and slide down towards lower ribs

lengthen spine and create space between the vertebrae

shoulders, elbows, wrists and fingers stacked

slight anterior tilt of pelvis

root down through four corners of feet (mound of big toe, mound of pinky toe, and both sides of heel)

press upwards through active feet

slight anterior tilt of pelvis

stack pelvis over shoulders

stack shoulders, elbows, wrists

root through full handprints

**Urdhva Vrkasana
(Upward Facing Tree/Handstand)**

71

BONE STACKING IN POSTURES

Utthita Chaturanga Dandasana
(High Plank)

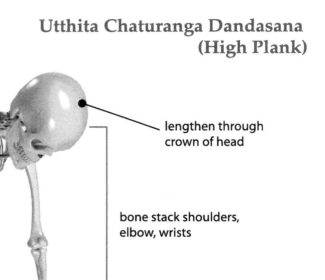

pelvis in line with
shoulders and heels

align hips, legs,
ankles, heels

lengthen through
crown of head

bone stack shoulders,
elbow, wrists

slight anterior
tilt of pelvis

heels stacked over toes

spread fingers wide, root
through full handprints

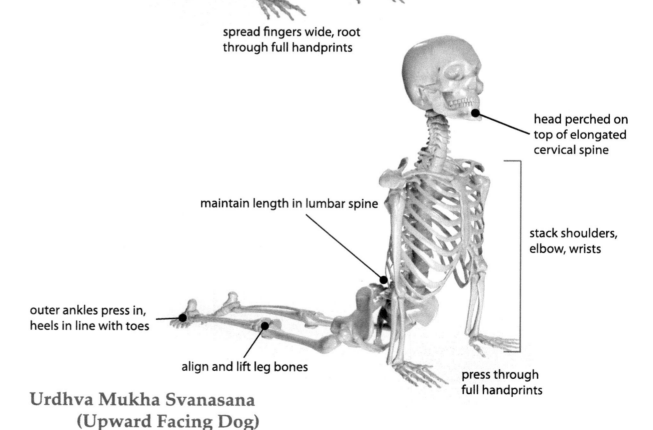

head perched on
top of elongated
cervical spine

maintain length in lumbar spine

stack shoulders,
elbow, wrists

outer ankles press in,
heels in line with toes

align and lift leg bones

press through
full handprints

Urdhva Mukha Svanasana
(Upward Facing Dog)

Virabhadrasana III
(Warrior 3)

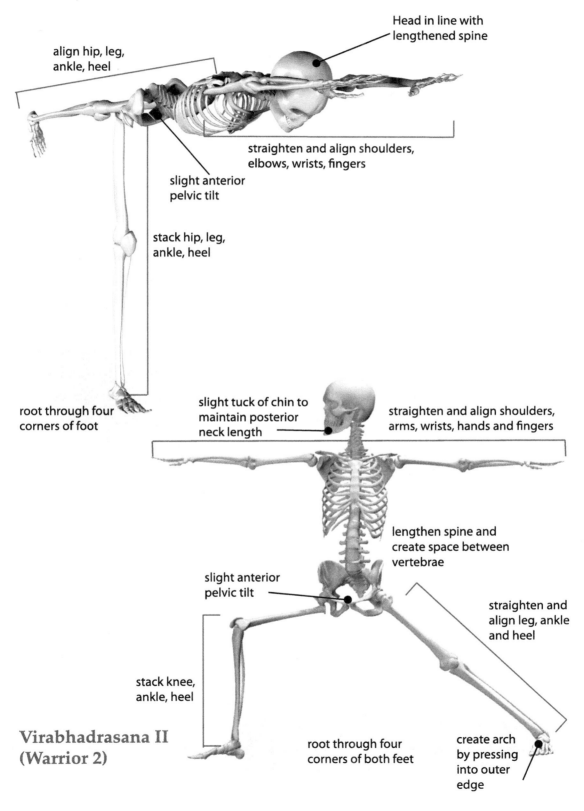

Head in line with lengthened spine

align hip, leg, ankle, heel

straighten and align shoulders, elbows, wrists, fingers

slight anterior pelvic tilt

stack hip, leg, ankle, heel

root through four corners of foot

slight tuck of chin to maintain posterior neck length

straighten and align shoulders, arms, wrists, hands and fingers

lengthen spine and create space between vertebrae

slight anterior pelvic tilt

straighten and align leg, ankle and heel

stack knee, ankle, heel

Virabhadrasana II
(Warrior 2)

root through four corners of both feet

create arch by pressing into outer edge

73

MUSCLE ACTIVATION AND JOINT MOVEMENT

There are over 700 muscles in the human body. There are 3 types of muscles: cardiac (heart), smooth (organs and vessels), and skeletal. The muscular-skeletal system, in addition to moving bones, gives shape and structure to the skeletal system. There are three types of contractions: concentric (bones move towards each other and angle of joint decreases), eccentric (bones move away from each other and the angle of the joint increase) and isometric (no movement of bones and joint is stabilized). The primary moving muscle of any joint is the agonistic muscle. It can only do its job efficiently and effectively if the opposing muscle, the antagonist muscle, relaxes. This is why yoga is so perfect for the body: strengthens AND stretches the muscles.

In addition to agonist and antagonist muscles, we have synergist and fixator muscles. Synergist muscles help support agonist muscles as they perform their prime moving of a joint. Both synergist muscles and fixator muscles work to stabilize the joint where prime movement is happening. During this prime movement, other fixator muscles in the body stabilize joints or body parts to reduce unnecessary movement in the non prime moving area.

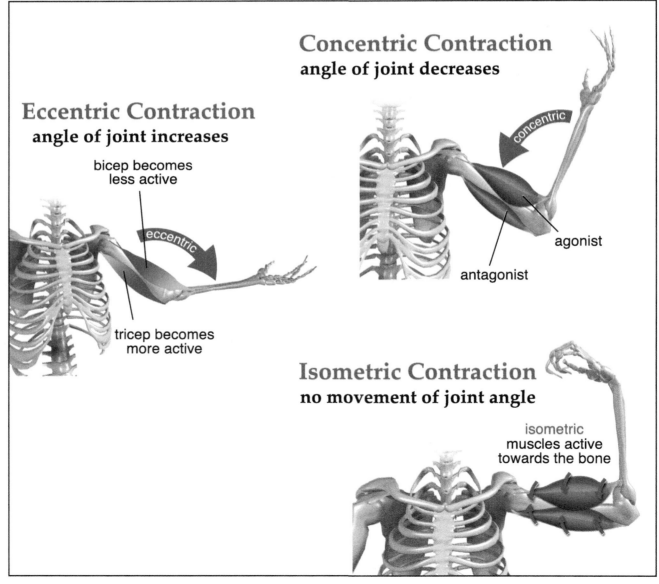

Concentric Contraction
angle of joint decreases

concentric

agonist

antagonist

Eccentric Contraction
angle of joint increases

bicep becomes
less active

eccentric

tricep becomes
more active

Isometric Contraction
no movement of joint angle

isometric
muscles active
towards the bone

MAJOR MUSCLES IN HUMAN BODY

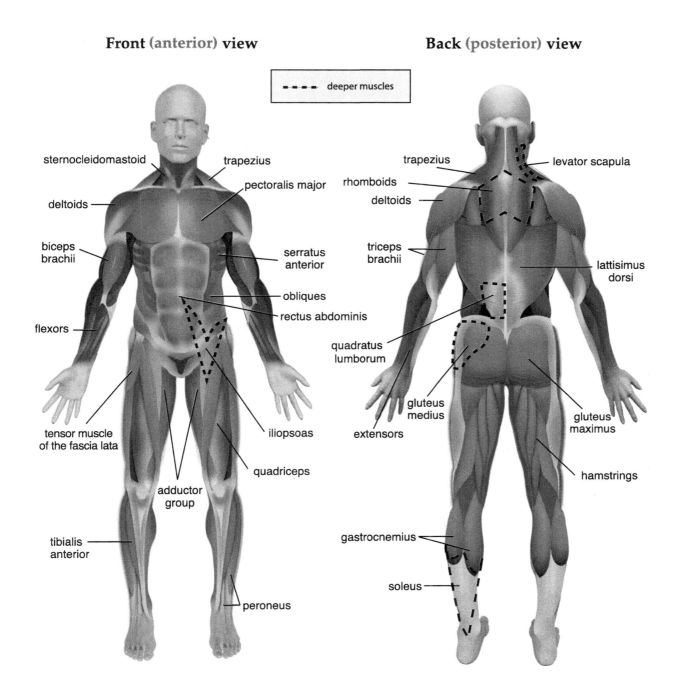

Front (anterior) view　　　　　　　**Back (posterior) view**

- - - - deeper muscles

Front (anterior) view labels:
sternocleidomastoid
trapezius
pectoralis major
deltoids
biceps brachii
serratus anterior
obliques
rectus abdominis
flexors
tensor muscle of the fascia lata
iliopsoas
adductor group
quadriceps
tibialis anterior
peroneus

Back (posterior) view labels:
trapezius
levator scapula
rhomboids
deltoids
triceps brachii
lattisimus dorsi
quadratus lumborum
gluteus medius
extensors
gluteus maximus
hamstrings
gastrocnemius
soleus

Deeper muscles not shown:

shoulder rotator cuff
(subscapularis, supraspinatus, infraspinatus, teres major & minor)
spinal column muscles
(erector spinae)
deep exeternal rotators of the hip
(piriformis, superior & inferior gamellus, obturator internus, quadratus femoris)

PLANES OF MOVEMENT

This perfect working organism of the human body moves through space and time in three different planes. The movements of flexion (forward) and extension (back) take place in the sagittal plane; abduction (away from the midline) and adduction (towards the midline) take place in the coronal plane; and rotation (twisting) takes place in the transverse plane. Most people spend their time operating in the sagittal plane - sitting at a desk, eating at a table, watching tv on couch, driving a car, riding a bike, running, hiking, rowing, etc. One of the many great things about practicing vinyasa flow yoga is that you can shift out of habitual patterns and conditioning by moving and playing in all three planes of movement.

Coronal Plane:
abduction and adduction

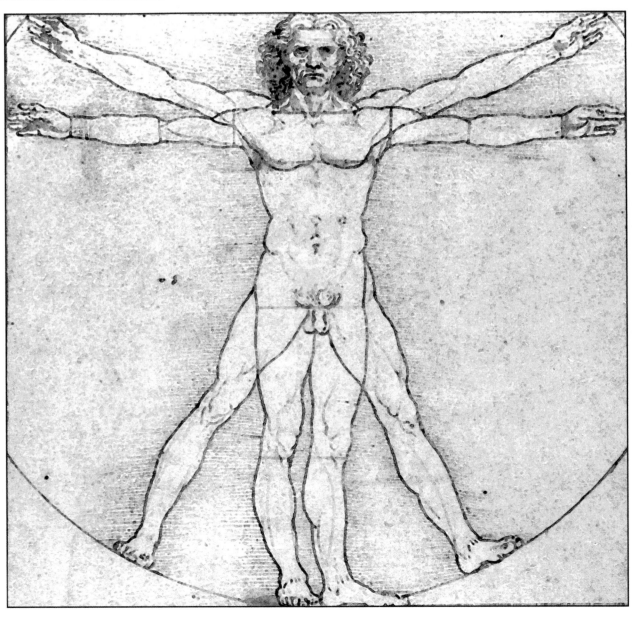

Sagittal Plane:
flexion and extension

Transverse Plane:
rotation

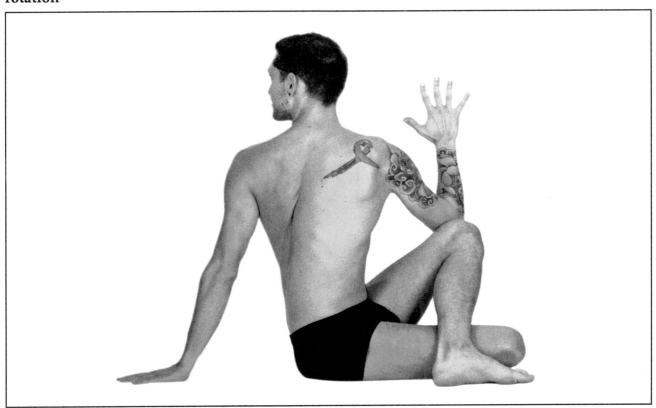

MAJOR JOINT MOVEMENTS IN THE HUMAN BODY

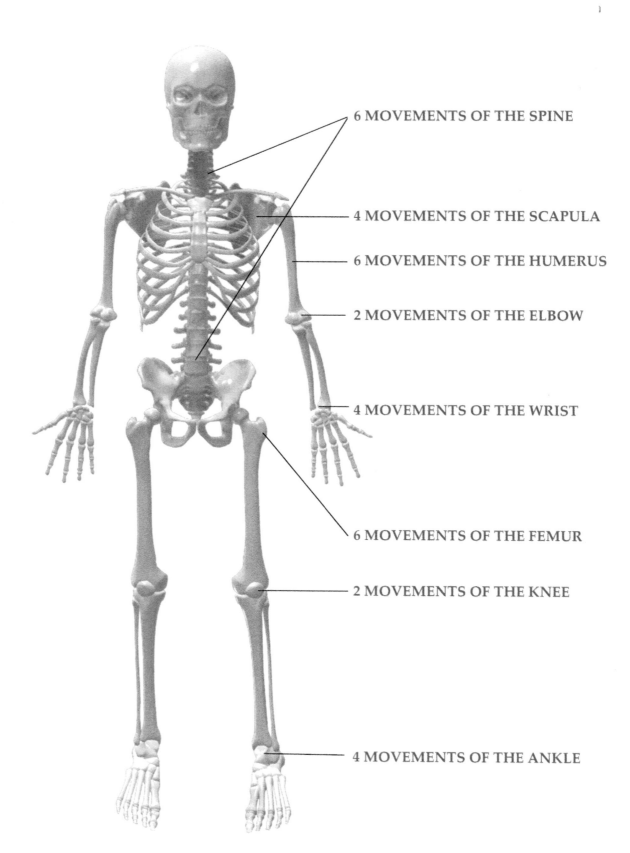

6 MOVEMENTS OF THE SPINE

4 MOVEMENTS OF THE SCAPULA

6 MOVEMENTS OF THE HUMERUS

2 MOVEMENTS OF THE ELBOW

4 MOVEMENTS OF THE WRIST

6 MOVEMENTS OF THE FEMUR

2 MOVEMENTS OF THE KNEE

4 MOVEMENTS OF THE ANKLE

MAJOR JOINT MOVEMENTS IN THE HUMAN BODY

6 Movements of the Spine

1. Neck and Torso Flexion
Marjaryasana (cat)

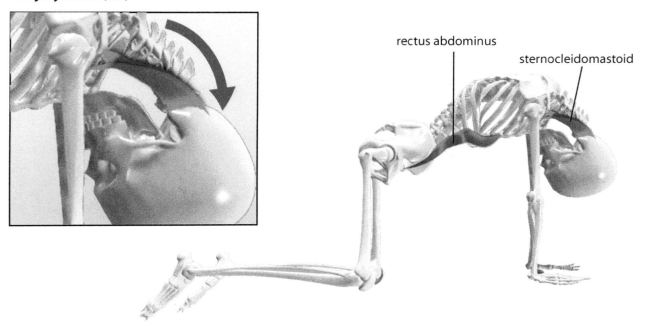

rectus abdominus

sternocleidomastoid

2. Neck and Torso Extension
Bitilasana (cow)

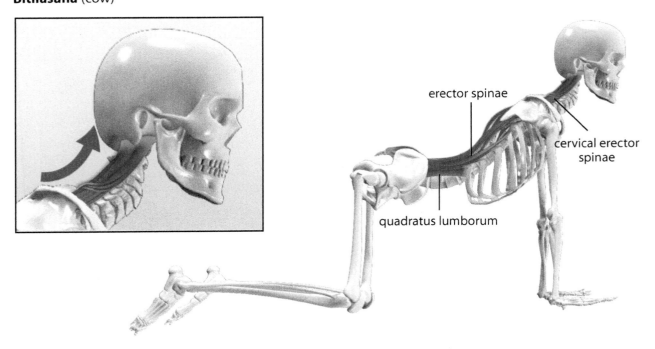

erector spinae

cervical erector spinae

quadratus lumborum

6 Movements of the Spine

Seated Side Bend

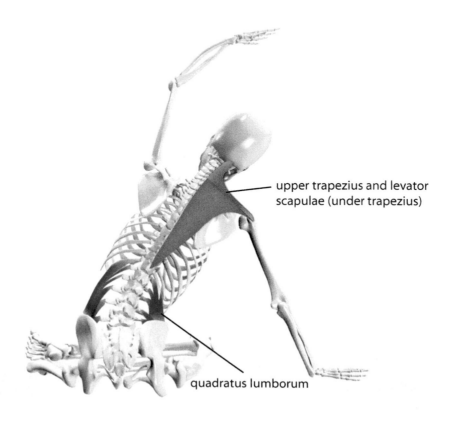

upper trapezius and levator scapulae (under trapezius)

quadratus lumborum

3. Torso Lateral Flexion

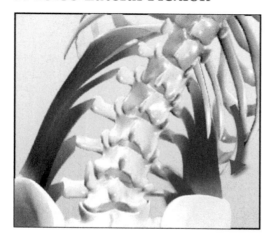

4. Neck Lateral Flexion

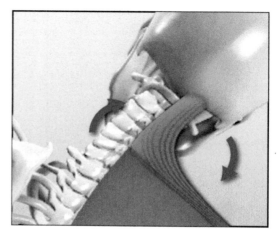

6 Movements of the Spine

Ardha Matsyendrasana
(half lord of the fishes pose)

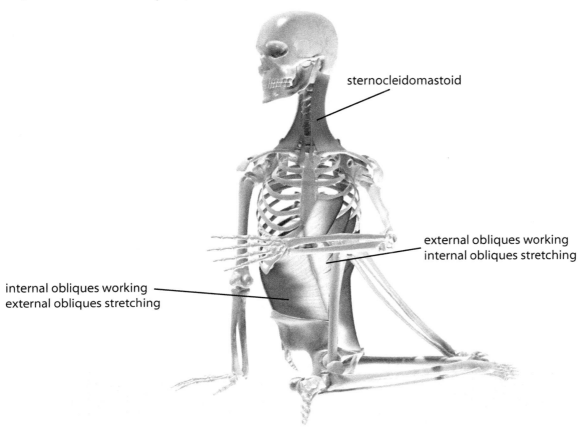

sternocleidomastoid

external obliques working
internal obliques stretching

internal obliques working
external obliques stretching

5. Neck Rotation

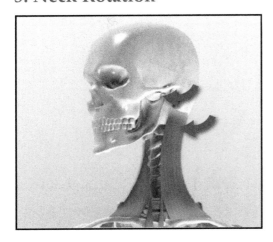

6. Torso Rotation

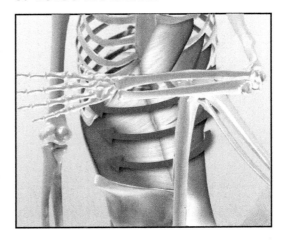

81

Shoulder Girdle

4 Movements of the Scapula

1. Scapula Elevation
Utthita Parighasana (extended side gate)

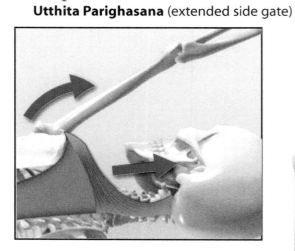

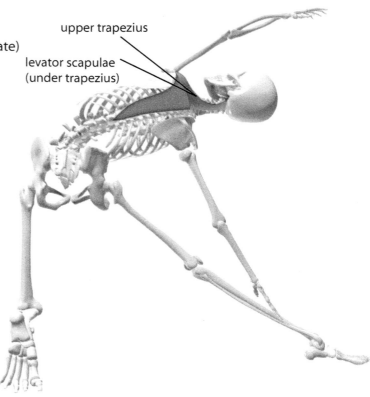

upper trapezius

levator scapulae
(under trapezius)

2. Scapula Depression
Tolasana (scale pose)

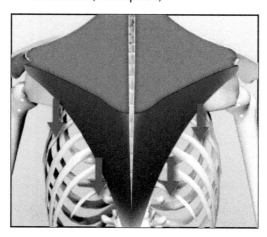

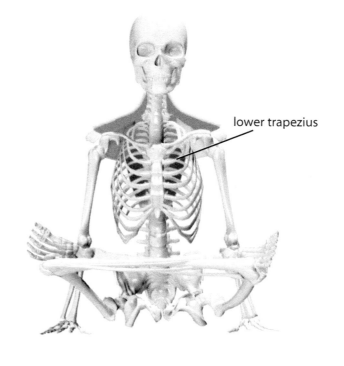

lower trapezius

4 Movements of the Scapula

3. Scapula Retraction
Seated cow with arms

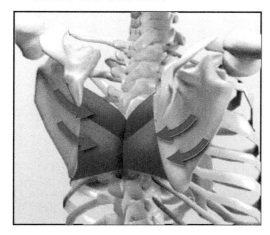

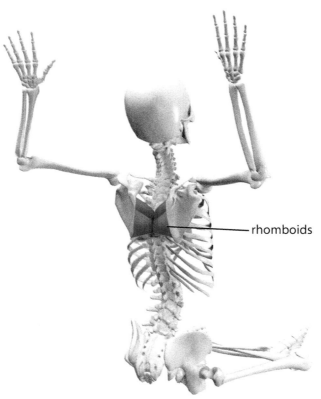

rhomboids

4. Scapula Protraction
Seated cat with arms

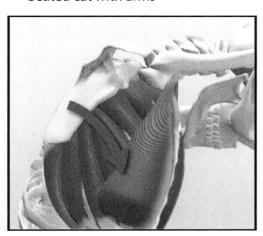

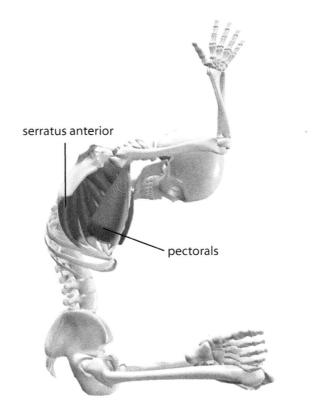

serratus anterior

pectorals

Shoulder Girdle

6 Movements of the Humerus

1. Shoulder Flexion
Utthita Chaturanga Dandasana (plank)

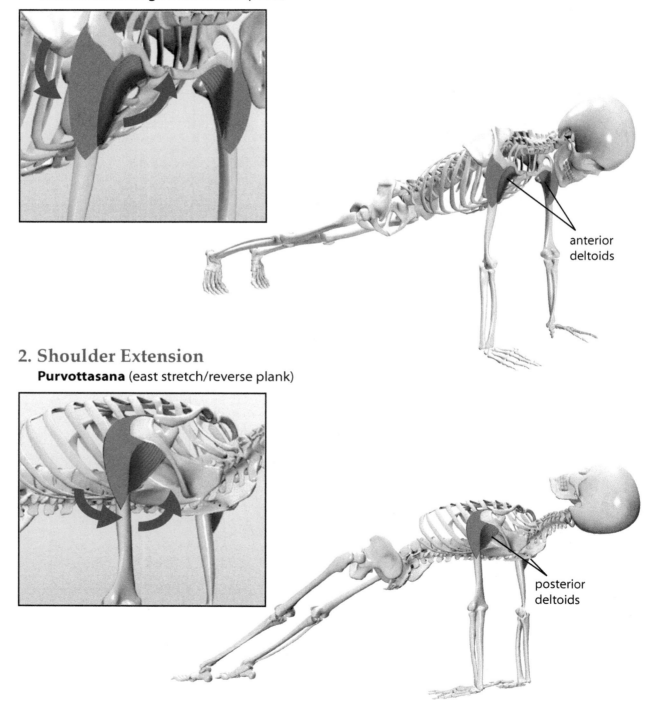

anterior
deltoids

2. Shoulder Extension
Purvottasana (east stretch/reverse plank)

posterior
deltoids

6 Movements of the Humerus

3. Shoulder Abduction
Vasisthasana (side plank)

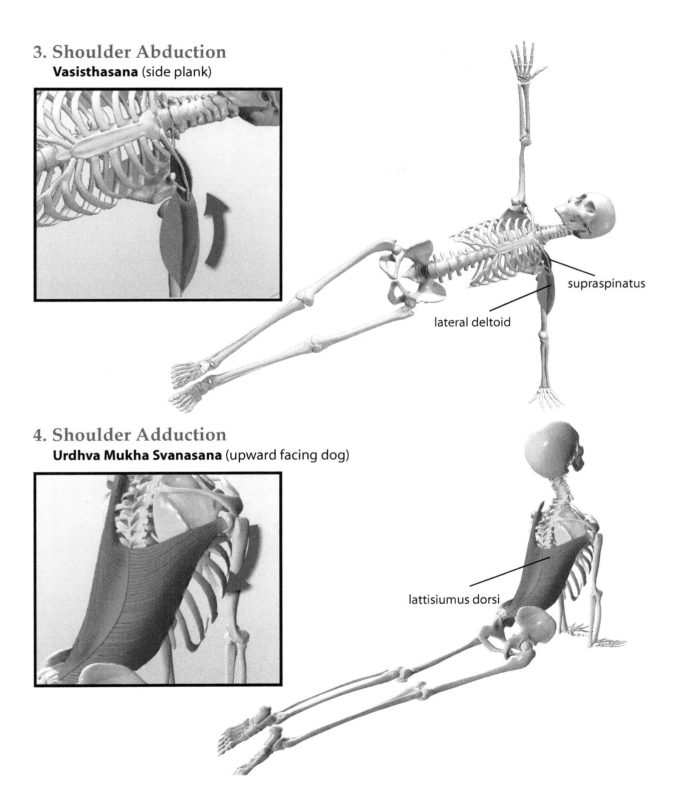

supraspinatus

lateral deltoid

4. Shoulder Adduction
Urdhva Mukha Svanasana (upward facing dog)

lattisiumus dorsi

Shoulder Girdle

6 Movements of the Humerus

5. Shoulder Internal Rotation
Gomukhasana (cow face pose)

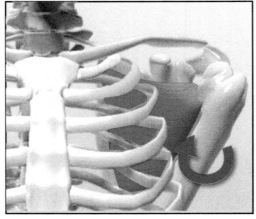

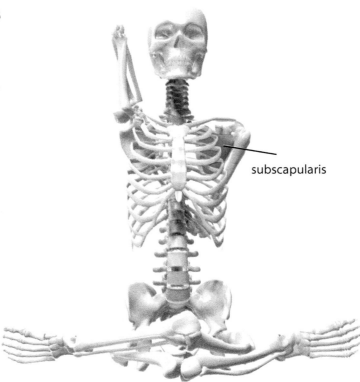

subscapularis

6. Shoulder External Rotation
Ghomukhasana (cow face pose)

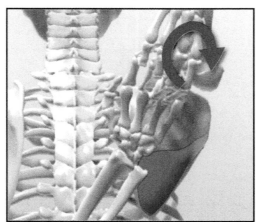

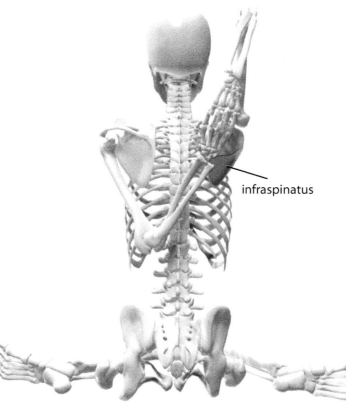

infraspinatus

Shoulder Girdle Extremities

2 Movements of the Elbow

1. Elbow Flexion
Mayurasana (peacock pose)

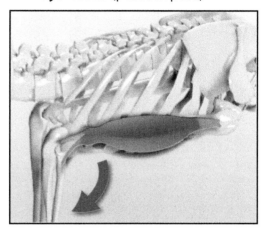

biceps

2. Elbow Extension
Dhanurasana (floor bow pose)

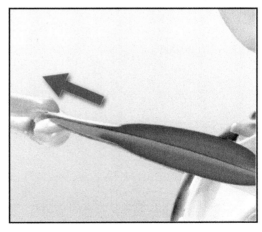

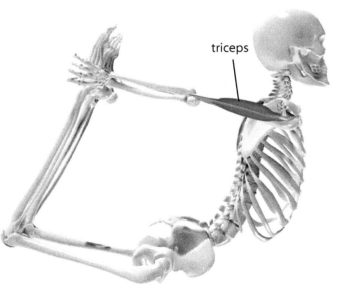

triceps

Shoulder Girdle Extremities

4 Movements of the Wrist

1. Wrist Flexion
Tabletop wrist stretch

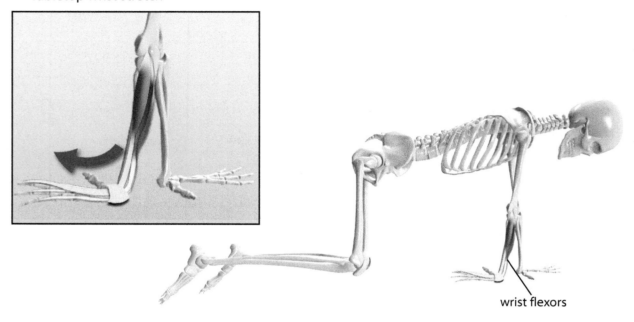

wrist flexors

2. Wrist Extension
Tabletop wrist stretch

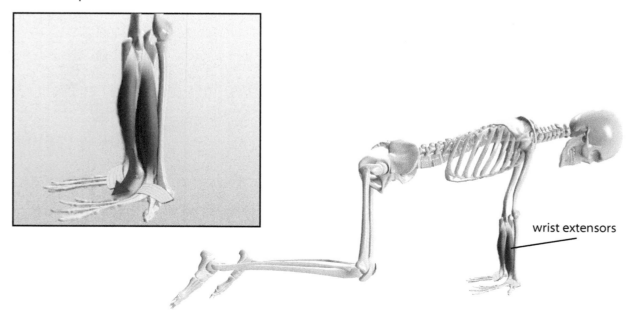

wrist extensors

4 Movements of the Wrist

3. Wrist Deviation, Ulnar
Waving Hand

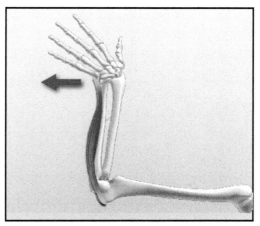

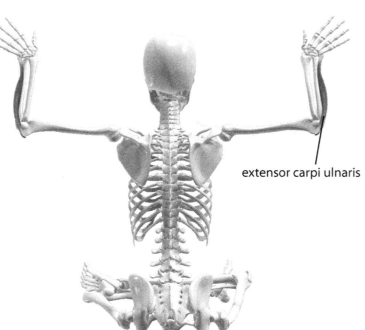

extensor carpi ulnaris

4. Wrist Deviation, Radial
Waving hand

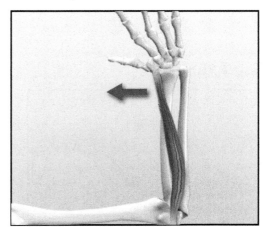

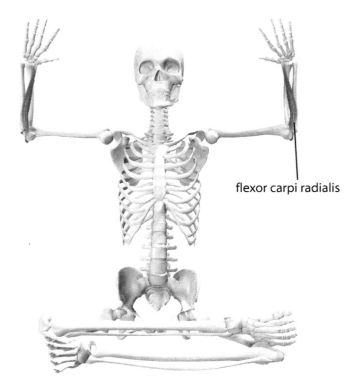

flexor carpi radialis

Hip Girdle

6 Movements of the Femur

Virabhadrasana III (warrior 3)

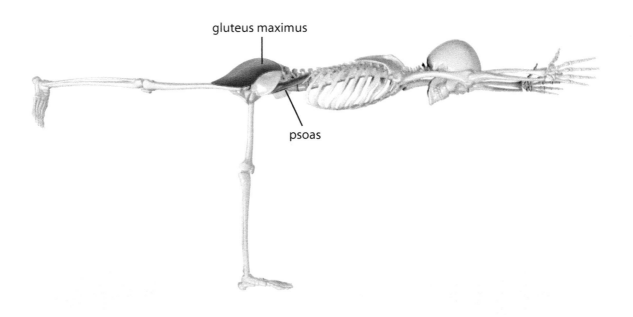

gluteus maximus

psoas

1. Hip Flexor

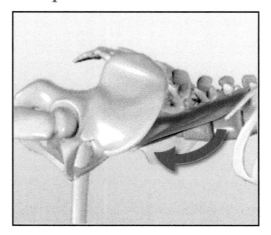

2. Hip Extensor

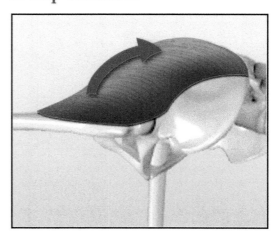

6 Movements of the Femur

3. Hip Abductor
Ardha Chandrasana (balancing half moon)

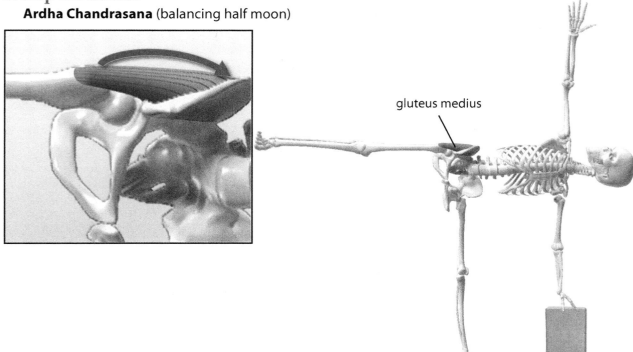

gluteus medius

4. Hip Adductor
Parsva Bakasana (extended side crow)

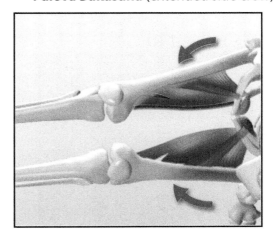

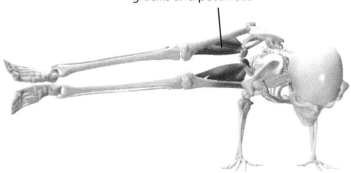

adductor group
-adductor magnus, longus and brevus
-gracilis and pectineus

6 Movements of the Femur

Mrigi Mudra (deer pose)

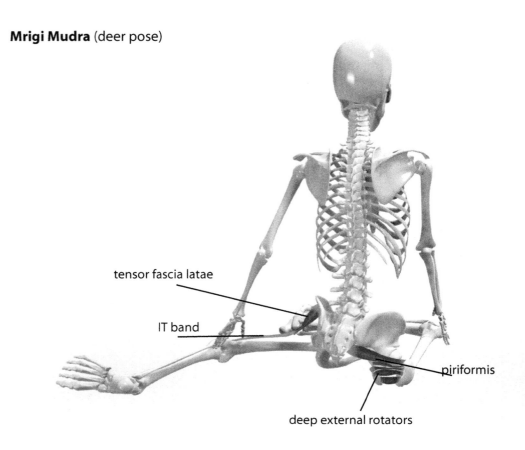

tensor fascia latae

IT band

piriformis

deep external rotators

5. Hip Internal Rotation

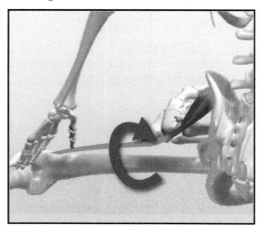

6. Hip External Rotation

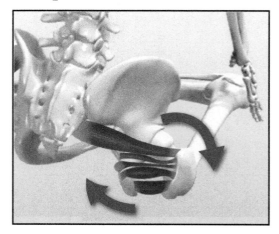

Hip Girdle Extremities

2 Movements of the Knee

Natarajasana (dancer's pose)

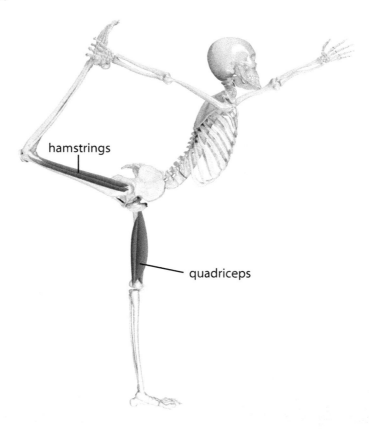

hamstrings

quadriceps

1. Knee Flexor

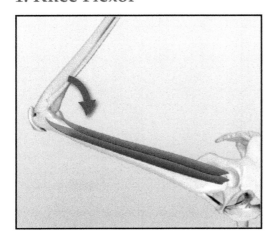

2. Knee Extensor

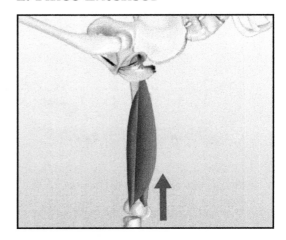

Hip Girdle Extremities

4 Movements of the Ankle

Flying Elephant Trunk Pose

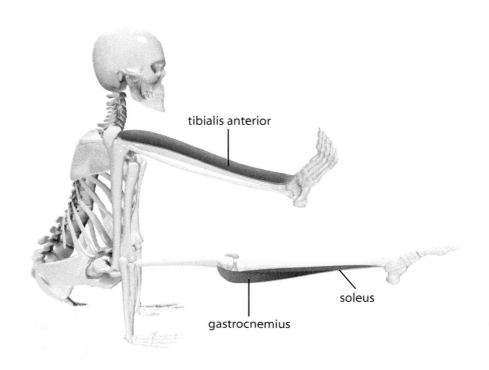

tibialis anterior

soleus

gastrocnemius

1. Ankle Flexion

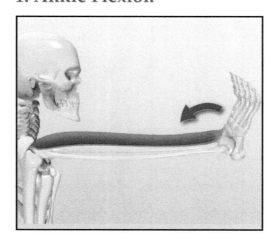

2. Ankle Extension

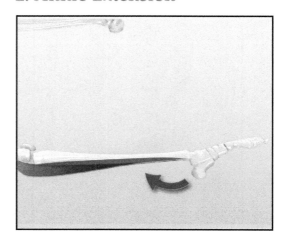

4 Movements of the Ankle

3. Ankle Inversion
Visvamitrasana (Sage Visvamitra pose)

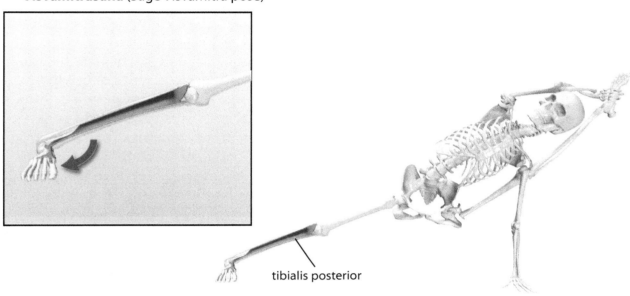

tibialis posterior

4. Ankle Eversion
Vasisthasana (Sage Vasisthasa pose)

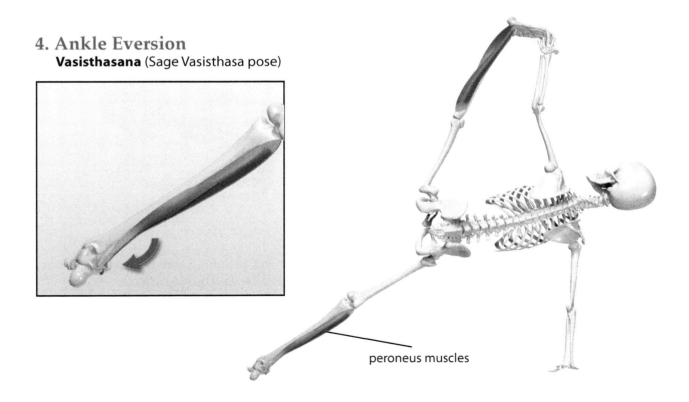

peroneus muscles

JOINT INTEGRATION & STABILIZATION

In order to prevent joint injuries while practicing vinyasa yoga, skeletal muscles need to be efficiently and effectively activated to stabilize bones in their joints. In order for this to be accomplished successfully, muscles need to be both strong and supple. Sage Patanjali wrote, *Sthira Sukham Asanam:* Slow and Steady in the Posture. After landing in a specific pose, a practitioner needs to scan his or her body, from foundation upward, and ask the question: "What muscles do I need to strengthen and what muscles do I need to soften in order to be able to hold this pose with ease?"

We use concentric and eccentric contraction to get in and out of poses, but it is the isometric contractions that keep us steady in the pose. Most yoga teachers will not use the words "isometric contraction" instead using a more yogic language like "wrap your muscles around your bones", "hug your muscles to the bones" and "spiral your muscles around your bones." If a practitioner knows and feels what muscles need to contract isometrically, in order to support the skeletal system in any given posture, he or she will foster an intimate awareness of muscle, bone and joint integration. This integration creates strong, supple and stabile joints which will ensure not only the longevity of your practice on the yoga mat, but the longevity of your life's practice of moving, playing, dancing and creating off the mat as well.

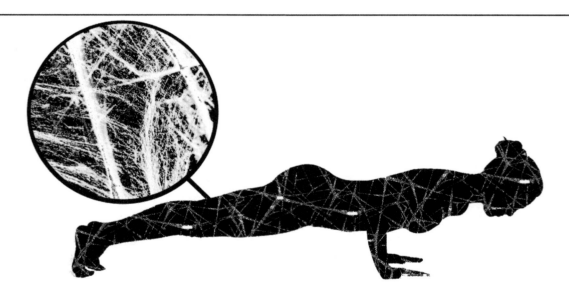

MYOFASCIA: THE ULTIMATE YOGIC CONNECTIVE TISSUE

In order to be completely integrated as a whole living, breathing, and moving human being, it is important to become attuned to the subtleties of myofascia (commonly referred to as fascia). Fascia is an intelligent, intricate web of connective tissue that weaves around everything in our bodies (muscles, organs and even the spaces in between). It is the glue that ultimately keeps us together. If tugged or pulled this matrix will drag everything it is attached to in the direction of that specific tug or pull. Fortunately, this organic compound, if supported and tended to with awareness, movement and massage, can keep our bodies radiantly healthy, supple and agile for a long lifetime.

THE NEXT THREE CHAPTERS

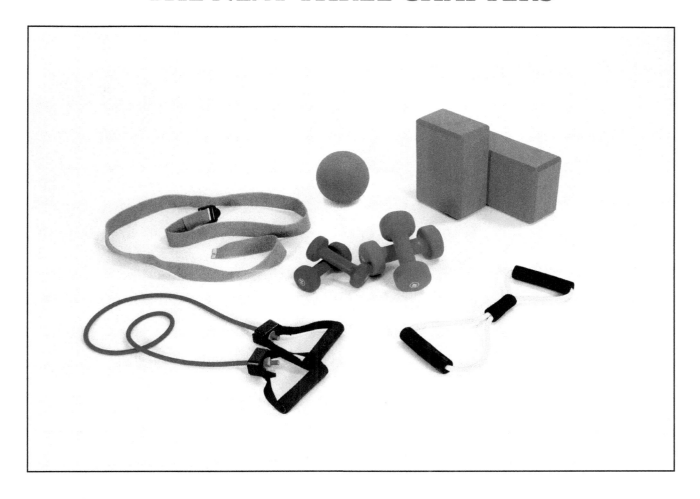

ON AND OFF THE MAT
TOOLS AND TECHNIQUES

In order to help strengthen and stretch the major muscles needed for chaturanga dandasana (four-limbed staff pose/low plank), urdhva mukha svanasana (upward facing dog) and adho mukha svanasana (downward facing dog) - the 3 most commonly practiced asanas in vinyasa flow yoga - the next three chapters will outline and illustrate both on and off the mat strengthening and stretching techniques.

Above accessories to aid in this quest:
2lb and/or 5lb hand weights, yoga strap, yoga blocks,
exercise bands with handles, and small exercise ball.

*Always check with your physician before starting any exercise program.

THE PERFECT CHATURANGA

Power is created in the mind,

rooted in the feet,

developed in the legs,

directed by the hips,

transfered through the torso,

focused on the feet or hands,

and felt in the spirit.

-unknown author

THE PERFECT CHATURANGA

I am standing tall and still in Tadasana, feeling rooted and grounded in my mountain pose. Inhaling I sweep my arms overhead, connecting the earth to the sky. Exhaling, I draw my hands down through my heart center, hinging forward at the hips, bowing to the awesome, brilliant, and undiscriminating sun. Fingertips touching floor on either side of my toes I inhale to lift my spine towards parallel, bowing deeper towards my shins as I exhale. Planting my hands on either side of my feet I step back into a high plank. I pause to breathe and be. I hear my heart beat. Scanning my body from head to toe, from bone to skin, I begin to adjust. I feel my muscles wrapping around my bones, doing the jobs they were intended to do. I bone stack my shoulders over elbows and wrists and extend the crown of my head towards the front of the mat, pressing the four corners of my feet towards the back. I actively wrap my shoulder blades onto my upper back. At the same time I send my shoulder blades and my tailbone towards my heels. My thigh muscles engage and lift my thigh bones and my abdominal muscles strengthen my core and support my spine. I can feel the muscles of my chest getting stronger and more defined as I hold myself here. Looking down at my hands I see my fingers spread wide, I know I am leaving two full handprints impressed into my mat. I check to feel the length of my neck, the space increasing between my ears and the tops of my shoulders. Once again I send my shoulder blades and tail to the back of my mat space. I am light here on my wrists and my toes. Stabilizing myself here I feel balanced. I connect to a deep sense of harmony and peace. I feel as though I can maintain this posture for a very long time, steady and comfortable, meditating on my breath. When the time is right, I listen and allow the next exhale to guide me into Chaturanga Dandasana. Looking towards the front of my mat in order to lead with my heart I feel my toes shift me forward slightly and I begin to lower down, elbows brushing past my ribcage, two 90 degree angles at my sides. I hold myself parallel to the earth. A bit more challenged I once again scan my body and make the same necessary adjustments as I did in plank. Starting at the soles of my feet I activate all the muscles needed to keep me feeling stable and light. Heels to the back, shins and thigh muscles holding legs parallel to the mat, tail towards my heels, abs and chest muscles strong, shoulders broad and away from my ears, shoulderblades broadened on my back, heading back towards my heels, neck long, heart buoyant in my chest as I look slightly forward. My victorious, ujjayi breath long and deep. I listen for my heart beating. Steady and comfortable, I wait.

Chaturanga Dandasana

Chatur - Four   **Anga** - Limb
Danda - Staff   **Asana** - Pose

High Plank

Energy Heels Back ⟵⟶ Energy Head Forward

Serratus Anterior Actively Keeping Shoulder Blades on Ribs

Lower Trapezius Actively Keeping Shoulders Away from Ears

Sending Tailbone Towards Heels

Gaze Slightly Forward, Neck Long

Heels Directly Over Spread Toes

Stacked Shoulders, Over Elbows, Over Wrists

Abdominals Actively Supporting Organs and Spine

Pectorals Active, Armpit Hollows

Tibialis Anterior Keeping Feet and Toes Flexed

Spread Fingers, Full Handprints, Pressing Earth Away

Quadriceps Lifting Thighs and Straightening Legs

Low Plank
Chaturanga Dandasana

Elbows 90 Degrees
(or close to it depending on proportion of arm bones)

Infraspinatus and
Lattisimus Dorsi
Draw Elbows In

Serratus Anterior
Spread Shoulder
Blades on Back

Long Neck

Lengthen Tail
Towards Heels

Gaze Slightly
Forward

Roll Shoulders
Away from Ears

Tibialis Anterior Continues
to Activate Even While
Calf Muscles Engage

Pectorals Active

Abdominal Muscles Active
Uddiyana Bandha
Actively Engaged

Ribcage Level with
Upper Arms

Toes Propelling Forward
(TOE YOGA!)

Quadriceps Active

POSE OF DYNAMIC EQUILIBRIUM

Chaturanga Dandasana (four-limbed staff pose) is a pose of perfect balance and symmetry. To find the sweet equipoise between the upper body muscles that push forward/press away (triceps, pectorals and serratus anterior) and the ones that pull back/draw towards (biceps, rhomboids and latissimus dorsi) a practitioner needs dedication to self-exploration, adherence to expert instruction, and diligent practice in order to refine and perfect.

PUSHING MUSCLES Pectoralis, Triceps, Serratus Anterior

PULLING MUSCLES Rhomboids, Trapezius, Latissimus Dorsi, Biceps

SIGNS OF IMBALANCE

Dipped Head

Winged Scapula

Wide Elbows

Dipped Hips

Rolled Out Hands

Muscles to Strengthen
- Erector Spinae
- Abdominals
- Serratus Anterior
- Lower Trapezius
- Latissiumus Dorsi
- Biceps
- Triceps
- Infraspinatus
- Quadriceps

Muscles to Stretch
- Erector Spinae
- Sternocleidomastoid
- Upper Trapezius
- Levator Scapula
- Subscapularis
- Quadratus Lumborum

SIGNS OF IMBALANCE

Shoulders Dip, Round &
Internally Rotate

Hips High

Knees Bent

Muscles to Strengthen

- Erector Spinae
- Rhomboids
- Mid/Lower Trapezius
- Infraspinatus
- Serratus anterior
- Quadratus Lumborum
- Gluteus Maximus
- Quadriceps
- Abdominals

Muscles to Stretch

- Pectorals
- Levator Scapula
- Upper trapezius
- Supraspinatus
- Subscapularis
- Hamstrings

SIGNS OF IMBALANCE

Shoulders to Ears

Thighs, Hips, and
Belly Collapse

Dipped Head

Muscles to Strengthen

- Erector Spinae
- Abdominals
- Iliopsoas
- Quadriceps
- Pectorals
- Anterior Deltoids
- Serratus Anterior

Muscles to Stretch

- Erector Spinae
- Sternocleidomastoid
- Upper Trapezius
- Levator Scapula
- Rear Deltoids
- Rhomboids
- Quadratus Lumborum
- Gluteus Maximus

ON THE MAT TOOLS AND TECHNIQUES TO STRENGTHEN YOUR CHATURANGA DANDASANA

KNEE DOWN PUSH UPS

Starting Position: Plank pose with shoulders over wrists. Lower knees gently to floor. Activate abdominal muscles as you maintain a straight line from crown to knees.

Practice Details: Keeping elbows tucked into side ribcage, exhale lower down to hover off floor (keeping upper arms parallel to the floor as much as possible). Draw your shoulder blades towards tailbone. Inhale, press the mat away as you straighten your elbows and broaden your shoulder blades across back.

Duration: 1-3 sets of ten repetitions.

Muscles Strengthened: Biceps, Triceps, Pectorals, Serratus Anterior, Rhomboids, Infraspinatus, Anterior Deltoid, Mid-Lower Trapezius, Abdominals

WEIGHTS FOR WRISTS

Starting Position: Take ahold of two 5lb weights (need the height of 5lb weights to slide knuckles under). Make your way into plank pose stacking shoulders over wrists. Engage abdominal muscles to support long line from crown to heels.

Practice Details: Keep carpal (wrist) bones perfectly stacked as you exhale to shift forward and lower whole body to hover over mat. Maintain stacked wrist bones as you inhale to press away from mat. This is also good for knee-down pushups and also, if core and upper body are strong, chaturanga to updog.

Duration: 1-3 sets of ten repetitions (or use throughout your flow practice if needed)

Muscles Strengthened: Biceps, Triceps, Pectorals, Serratus Anterior, Rhomboids, Infraspinatus, Anterior Deltoid, Mid-Lower Trapezius, Abdominals

*Reminds carpal bones of their weight bearing capacity.

YOGA BLOCKS

Starting Position: In plank, place two blocks underneath body (one an inch in front of fingertips and the other 6-8 inches behind it). Make sure your shoulders are stacked over wrists and heels over toes.

Practice Details: Inhale, shift forward with your toe strength and suppleness. Exhale, lower down your whole body to hover and, if needed, land lightly on blocks with your sternum (breastbone) and abdominal region. Keep your gaze slightly forward, shoulder blades drawn away from ears and widened towards outer ribs, elbows tucked in to ribs, draw your tail towards heels, activate abs, thigh and shin muscles, and flex toes. When finished, press up and back to downward facing dog.

Duration: 1-5 repetitions daily until strong enough for chaturanga dandasana.

Muscles Strengthened: Biceps, Triceps, Pectorals, Serratus Anterior, Rhomboids, Infraspinatus, Mid-Lower Trapezius, Abdominals, Quadriceps, Anterior Tibialis

YOGA STRAP

Starting Position: Create a loop with yoga strap, wrap above the elbow crease (shoulder width apart) with buckle not touching skin. Find yourself in plank position, shoulders over elbows over wrists and heels over toes

Practice Details: Inhale, toes propel you forward in plank. Exhale, lower down and rest your ribcage lightly on strap. Gaze slightly forward, shoulders broad and drawn away from ears, tail towards heels, abs and thighs active. When finished, press up and back to downward facing dog.

Duration: 1-5 repetitions daily until strong enough for chaturanga dandasana.

Muscles Strengthened: Biceps, Triceps, Pectorals, Serratus Anterior, Rhomboids, Infraspinatus, Mid-Lower Trapezius, Abdominals, Quadriceps, Anterior Tibialis

DOLPHIN PUSH-UPS

Starting position: From tabletop position lower down on to forearms and either interlace fingers or flatten palms on mat. Maintain shoulder distance between elbows. Curl your toes under, lift hips and start to straighten knees into dolphin posture.

Practice Details: Inhale, shift forward from dolphin to a forearm plank. Keep your neck in a straight line, gaze slightly forward. Use your chaturanga cues here…no sinking towards floor with chest or hips. Inhale, lift hips back into dolphin. Continue lowering and lifting body with breath. Make sure to not let shoulders go forward of hands in forearm plank.

Duration: 1-3 sets of 10 repetitions.

Muscles Strengthened: Pectorals, Anterior and Posterior Deltoids, Trapezius, Latissiumus Dorsi, Serratus Anterior, Rhomboids, Infraspinatus

SHOULDER BLADE FLOSSING

Starting Position: Forearm plank position with hands either interlaced or palms flat in line with elbow creases (elbows are directly under shoulders). Make sure to keep body in one long line, actively engaging front body muscles to support body weight. You can lower knees to floor if needed.

Practice Details: Inhale slowly and with awareness, release chest slightly lower than shoulders, allowing shoulder blades to come together on back towards spinal column. Exhale, engage abdominals, press through forearms and dome upper back, spreading shoulder blades apart and wrapping shoulder blades onto outer ribs. With a slow and steady breath, go back and forth between two postures. Make sure to feel which muscles are strengthening.

Duration: 1-3 sets of 10 repetitions.

Muscles Strengthened: Serratus Anterior, Pectorals, Infraspinatus, Rhomboids, Trapezius

OFF THE MAT TOOLS AND TECHNIQUES TO STRENGTHEN YOUR CHATURANGA DANDASANA

BICEPS CURLS

Starting Position: Take a hold of a 1-5lb weight in either hand. Keep elbows slightly bent. Standing in mountain pose, softly bend knees. Maintain this slight bend. Engage abdominal muscles, lowering tailbone towards the earth. Draw shoulder blades back and down away from ears. Turn palms / weights towards mirror and keep bent elbows close to side waist.

Practice Details: Inhale, hinge right elbow bringing weight to your shoulder. Exhale slowly to extend at elbow joint (maintaining a slight bend at end of movement.) Repeat with left arm.

Duration: 1-3 sets of 10 repetitions on each side.

Muscles strengthened: Biceps

TRICEPS KICKBACKS

Starting Position: Take a hold of a 1-5lb weight in each hand. Keep elbows slightly bent. Standing in mountain pose, slightly bend knees and hinge forward at hips (45 degree angle). Engage abdominal muscles to support spine. Draw navel to spine each exhale. Turn palms / weights toward outer thighs and bend elbows to a 90 degree angle. Keeping elbows tucked in towards body, lift elbows behind torso so upper arms are parallel to the floor.

Practice Details: Inhale, slowly unhinge elbows and press the weights behind you. Exhale just as slowly to hinge elbows, drawing weights back towards ribs. After ten repetitions, exhale hinge elbows and inhale press through feet to stand up on mountain pose.

Duration: 1-3 sets of 10 repetitions.

Muscles Strengthened: Triceps, Abdominals

ANTERIOR DELTOID RAISES

Starting Position: Take a hold of a 1-5lb weight in either hand. Keep elbows slightly bent. Standing in mountain pose, softly bend knees. Maintain this slight bend. Engage abdominal muscles, lowering tailbone towards the earth. Draw scapula (shoulder blades) back and down away from ears. Turn palms/weights towards the front of thighs.

Practice Details: Initiating movement from the front of shoulder, inhale and slowly lift right arm in front until it is at shoulder height (maintain slight bend at elbow). Exhale, slowly lower and return arm to side. Repeat with left arm.

Duration: 1-3 sets of 10 repetitions on each side.

Muscles Strengthened: Anterior deltoids

RECLINING ANTERIOR DELTOID RAISES

Starting Position: Lie on your back with knees bent, feet on floor hips width apart. Take a hold of a 1-5lb weight in either hand and turn wrists so that thumbs are to the ceiling. Slightly bend elbows and hover arms over the mat about an inch.

Practice Details: Inhale, lift right arm towards the ceiling and towards the floor over the head. Maintain a slight bend in the elbow and only go as far as your shoulder range of motion will let you. Exhale, lower arm to hover by right side body. Repeat with left arm.

Duration: 1-3 sets of 10 repetitions on each side.

Muscles Strengthened: Anterior Deltoids

CHEST PRESS

Starting Position: Lie on back with knees bent, feet on floor hips width apart. Take a hold of a 1-5lb weight in either hand. Hinge elbows to 90 degrees and abduct upper arms out to either side palms/ weights face towards knees. Lift elbows an inch off floor.

Practice details: Inhale, slowly press weights towards ceiling. Exhale, slowly lower arms until elbows are hovering an inch off floor. After ten repetitions, draw weights in towards chest before next set.

Duration: 1-3 sets of 10 repetitions.

Muscles Strengthened: Pectorals, Deltoids, Triceps

PECTORAL FLIES

Starting Position: Lie on back with knees bent, feet on floor hips width apart. Take a hold of a 1-5lb weight in either hand. Bend elbows to 90 degrees. Reach both weights to the ceiling and let them touch.

Practice Details: Exhale, lower arms out to sides maintaining a slight bend at elbows. To avoid overstretching in pectoralis region, do not touch the floor with weighted hands. Inhale, lift weights towards ceiling until they touch. After ten repetitions, hug weights to chest before next set.

Duration: 1-3 sets of 10 repetitions.

Muscles Strengthened: Pectorals

ROTATOR CUFF STRENGTHENING (INTERNAL)

Starting Position: Stand in mountain pose, softly bent knees, abs activated, tailbone towards floor. Make sure resistance band is tied/attached securely to doorknob. Take ahold of the one handle end of band. Elbow of working rotator cuff is bent at 90 degrees, tucked into side waist. For internal rotation of RIGHT shoulder, band is in right hand, right hip near door.

Practice Details: For internal rotation: Inhale, slowly bring hand and band across lower belly towards opposite hip against resistance of band. Exhale, slowly return back to starting position. After ten repetitions slowly return back to starting position and safely release band. DO NOT LET BAND SNAP OUT OF HANDS OR OFF DOORKNOB.

Duration: 1-3 sets of 10 repetitions each side.

Muscles Strengthened: Internal Rotator (Subscapularis), Pectorals

ROTATOR CUFF STRENGTHENING (EXTERNAL)

Starting Position: Stand in mountain pose, softly bent knees, abs activated, tailbone towards floor. Make sure resistance band is tied/attached securely to doorknob. Take ahold of one handle end of band. Elbow of working rotator cuff is bent at 90degrees, tucked into side waist. For external rotation of RIGHT shoulder, band in left hand, right hip near door.

Practice Details: For external rotation: Inhale, draw hand and band across lower belly to forearms distance in front of hip keeping forearm parallel to floor. Exhale, slowly return back to starting position. After ten repetitions, slowly return to center and safely release band. DO NOT LET BAND SNAP OUT OF HANDS OR OFF DOORKNOB.

Duration: 1-3 sets of 10 repetitions each side.

Muscles Strengthened: External Rotator (Infraspinatus), Rhomboids

WRIST YOGA

Carpal (wrist) bones are short bones meant for weight bearing. This is good news for vinyasa yoga students who practice many chaturanga dandasanas, upward facing and downward facing dogs. If only it were that simple; the reality of the situation is that most adults have not been on their wrists since crawling, gymnastics, wrestling, break-dancing, etc. Additionally, we have imprinted our wrists with habitual patterns from decades of computer work. As a result, many new-to-vinyasa-yoga wrists may not be ready for so many weight bearing postures. In order to prevent injury, wrists need to be re-trained to be once again weight bearing.

STRENGTHEN:

Wrist Flexion

Wrist Extension

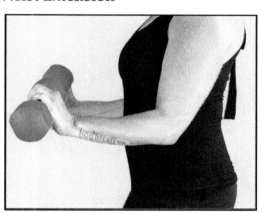

HASTA BANDHA: Happy Wrists

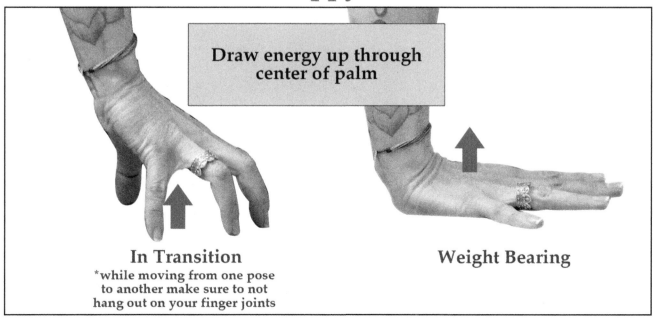

Draw energy up through center of palm

In Transition
*while moving from one pose to another make sure to not hang out on your finger joints

Weight Bearing

TOE YOGA

Ideally, it is desirable for all joints to be both strong and supple...even the toe joints. Increasing the range of motion in your toes will increase your ease as you propel yourself forward to lower in chaturanga dandasana and as you roll over your toes for both upward facing dog and downward facing dog. Until the toes are supple enough there is always the choice in the transition from chaturanga dandasana to upward facing dog to flip one foot over at a time – as long as you maintain level hips and active inner legs from arches to groin.

SUPPLE TOES

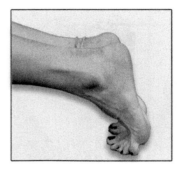

Shift forward in plank to lower down into chaturanga dandasana.

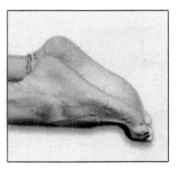

Energetically press toes back as you roll forward over them for upward facing dog.

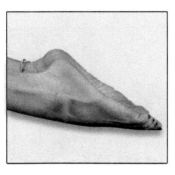

Lift hips and roll over toes to downward facing dog.

UNTIL TOES ARE READY TO ROLL

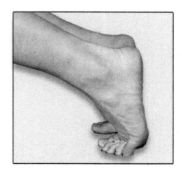

Shift forward in plank to lower down into chaturanga dandasana.

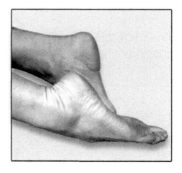

Maintain level hips as you lift one foot to flip onto top of foot (activate inner legs from arches to groin)

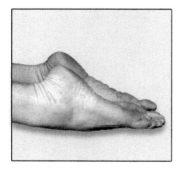

Maintain level hips as you flip other foot to meet in upward facing dog.

SUPPLE TOES PREPARATION

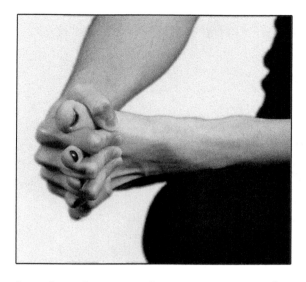

Interlace fingers in between toes and massage/rotate.

Curl toes under and sit on heels in kneeling posture, heels and arches towards each other.

PADA BANDHA: Happy Toes

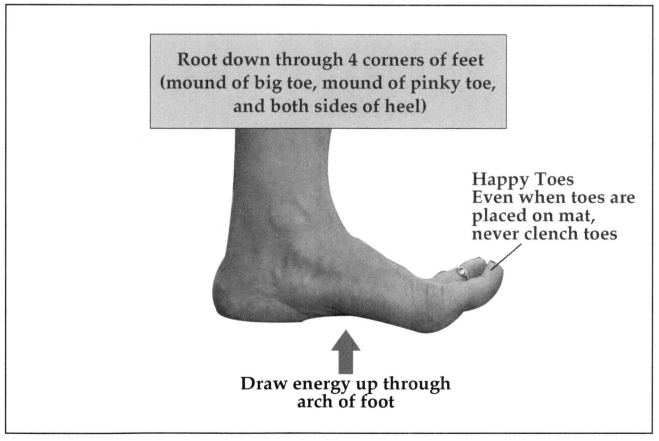

Root down through 4 corners of feet (mound of big toe, mound of pinky toe, and both sides of heel)

Happy Toes
Even when toes are placed on mat, never clench toes

Draw energy up through arch of foot

UPWARD FACING DOG

Sisters and brothers,

remember this:

the light of the sun-

warm, vibrant, and

radiant

shines even brighter

here on this earth

from the depths

of our open hearts.

-Jennilee

UPWARD FACING DOG

When the time is right, I inhale to propel myself forward from my Perfect Chaturanga pressing myself away from Mother Earth into Urdhva Mukha Svanasana, Upward Facing Dog. I feel my fingers are spread wide, leaving full handprints on my mat. As I bone stack my shoulders over my elbows and wrists, I roll my shoulders back and down, encouraging the shoulders blades closer together so that they can press into and lift my ribcage, supporting the opening of my heart. I keep my neck long. My drishti, my gaze, is forward and up and is being initiated from my heart's expansion. Deep breaths expand and contract my lungs, removing Dukkha (stale stagnate energy) and replacing it with Sukkha (sweet, pure energy.) I become acutely aware of the space between my ribs and my hips, knowing I am creating necessary space for my organs to optimally thrive. I breathe Prana, life force energy, into these spaces I am creating. I take a moment to scan my lower body...my hips, thighs, knees and ankles are lifted off the mat as I press firmly into the tops of my feet. I press my outer ankles in, maintaining long lines of energy from hips to toes. With my ujjayi breath I return my awareness to my active hands and spread fingers pressing the earth away and scan my entire body again, encouraging a fuller expression of this back body strengthening and front body opening pose. Encouraging an open heart I feel myself expanding and shining bright I listen for my heart beating. Steady and comfortable, I wait.

Urdhva Mukha Svanasana

Urdhva - Upward   **Mukha** - Facing
Svana - Dog   **Asana** - Pose

Upward Facing Dog Prep Pose
Bhujangasana Cobra Pose

Gaze is Forward and Slightly Lifted

Keep Back of Neck Long

Shoulders Rolled Back and Down

Lengthen Lower Back

Toned Buttocks

Align Hips, Knees, Ankles and Toes in Straight, Parallel Lines

Sternum Forward

Ribs Forward

Spread Fingers

Press into Tops of Feet

Kneecaps Lifted off Floor

Hips Rooted

Elbows Bent, Tucked to Sides and Drawn Towards Hips

"Scrubbing" hands back (slight pull towards back of mat)

Upward Facing Dog

Mid and Lower Trapezius Roll Shoulders Back and Down

Rhomboids Retract Shoulder Blades Supporting Lift of Ribcage

Space Between Ribs and Hips, Long Lower Back

Toned Gluteus and Hamstring Muscles Extend Hips (Careful not to Clench)

Long Neck, Gaze Lifted

Heart Opened, Chest Expanded

Shoulders Bonestacked Over Wrists

Spread Fingers, Full Handprints, Pressing Earth Away

Shins, Knees, and Thighs Off the Mat

Abdominals Engaged

Lattisimus Dorsi Drawing Arms into Sides

Pressing on Tops of Feet

SIGNS OF IMBALANCE

Head Fallen Back

Sunken Head into Shoulders

Bent Elbows to the Side

Rolled Out Hands

Muscles to Strengthen

- Sternocleidomastoid
- Rhomboids
- Mid/Lower Trapezius
- Latissimus Dorsi
- Infraspinatus
- Rear Deltoids
- Triceps
- Abdominals

Muscles to Stretch

- Erector Spinae
- Levator Scapula
- Upper Trapezius
- Subscapularis
- Biceps
- Quadratus Lumborum

SIGNS OF IMBALANCE

Rounded Shoulders to Ears

Bent Elbows

Wide Legs

Hips and Knees on Floor

Sickled Feet

Muscles to Strengthen

- Rhomboids
- Mid/Lower Trapezius
- Latissimus Dorsi
- Rear Deltoids
- Infraspinatus
- Triceps
- Quadratus Lumborum

- Gluteus Maxim
- Posterior Gluteus Medius
- External Rotators
- Quadriceps
- Adductor Group
- Tibialis Anterior
- Perroneus'

Muscles to Stretch

- Pectorals
- Upper Trapezius
- Levator Scapula
- Subscapularis
- Biceps
- Tensor Fascia Lata
- Anterior Gluteus Medius
- Hamstrings

ON THE MAT POSES TO STRENGTHEN YOUR UPWARD FACING DOG

SPHINX

Starting Position: Lying prone with hips, knees, ankles and toes aligned in a straight line.

Practice Details: Feeling the weight of your pubis and hips bones, exhale root down and anchor both. Inhale, peel yourself off the mat with your arm and back strength. Exhale, place elbows underneath shoulders (90 degree angle), spread fingertips are directly in front of elbow creases. Inhale, roll your shoulders back and down and send your sternum and ribs forward, maintaining length in the neck and shining continuously out through the crown of your head. Exhale, feel free to close your eyes as you experience lengthening in lower, mid and upper back. Inhale for length and strength. When done, exhale to lower to starting position, resting head on stacked forearms.

Duration: 10-20 long, slow, even breaths in and out through the nose.

Muscles strengthened: Erector Spinae, Back Extensors, Rhomboids, Mid and Lower Trapezius

LOCUST WITH HANDS CLASPED

Starting Position: Lying prone with straight legs either zipped together or separated hips width apart. If it's in your practice, draw shoulder blades together and interlace hands behind you at lower back. If shoulder mobility is restricted, have arms by your sides or use a strap between your hands.

Practice Details: Engaging your back body muscles, inhale to take flight, lifting your upper and lower body off the mat. Exhale, keep your neck long (no wrinkles behind your neck!) and make sure legs and arms are as straight as possible. Lift interlaced knuckles off your tailbone. With each inhale lift your upper and lower body higher off the mat. Each exhale simply stay and enjoy defying gravity! Lift to your highest point with one last inhale and then exhale to lower to starting position.

Duration: 10 slow, deep, energizing breaths in and out through the nose.

Muscles Strengthened: Erector Spinae, Back Extensors, Rhomboids, Gluteus Maximus, Hamstrings

FLOOR SWIMMING I

Starting Position: Lie on belly with arms stretched forward shoulders width apart. Keep legs straight and hips width apart behind you. Maintain a long straight neck with head lifted off the mat slightly.

Practice Details: Inhale, lift left arm and right leg off mat 1-4 inches. Exhale place back down. Inhale, lift right arm and left leg off mat 1-4 inches. Exhale place back down.

Duration: 1-3 sets of 10 repetitions.

Muscles Strengthened: Anterior Deltoids, Back Extensors, Erector Spinae, Gluteus Maximus, Hamstrings

FLOOR SWIMMING II

Starting Position: Lie on belly with arms by sides. Bring legs together behind you with inner thighs, knees, heels and big toes touching. Maintain a long straight neck with head lifted slightly off mat.

Practice Details: Inhale draw fingertips alongside body towards head and as if taking off a tophat reach arms long. Exhale, sweep arms out to sides and return to starting position. Maintain the lift of upper and lower body throughout the movement.

Duration: 1-3 sets of ten repetitions.

Muscles Strengthened: Back Extensors, Erector Spinae, Trape(s)ius, Latissimus Dorsi

OFF THE MAT TOOLS AND TECHNIQUES TO STRENGTHEN UPWARD FACING DOG

OVERHEAD TRICEP EXTENSION

Starting Position: Seated or Standing with bent knees.

Practice Details: Picking up one 2-5lb weight in right hand, bring weight close to chest before pressing it overhead, keeping weight, wrist, elbow and shoulder stacked. Support your right elbow with guidance from your left hand. Exhale, slowly use you bicep to hinge your right elbow joint and lower the weight to just behind the top of your head. Inhale engage triceps muscle to slowly press the weight back up to starting position. After ten repetitions, bring weight slowly down to chest and change hands. Repeat on other side.

Duration: 1-3 sets of 10 repetitions on each side.

Muscles Strengthened: Triceps

LAT PULL DOWN (WITH BAND)

Starting Position: Seated or Standing with bent knees.

Practice Details: Hold the handles of the exercise band overhead. With elbows slightly bent throughout exercise, exhale and slowly pull right handle of band out and down to the right with right hand (elbow will touch side waist). Just as slowly inhale the right hand back up to meet the left. Slowly and with control lower and lift ten times. After ten, return the right hand up to meet the left and change.

Duration: 1-3 sets of 10 repetitions on each side.

Muscles Strengthened: Latissimus Dorsi

ROWING

Starting Position: Sit with upright spine and extended legs in Dandasana (staff pose). Wrap a resistance band twice around your feet (so it does not roll off). Make sure you have two equal length "tails" of band. Wrap ends of resistance band twice around hands (don't let go). With elbows slightly bent turn palms to face each other.

Practice Details: Inhale, pull back slowly on bands as you squeeze your shoulder blades together. At the end of the movement elbows will be at 90 degrees by your ribs. Exhale, slowly return to starting position. After ten repetitions slowly return to starting position. ALWAYS MAINTAIN CONTROL OF PHYSIOBAND-NEVER LET IT SNAP OUT OF YOUR HANDS.

Duration: 1-3 sets of 10 repetitions.

Muscles Strengthened: Rhomboids

LEG EXTENSIONS

Starting Position: Sitting in chair. Hold sides of chair lightly with both hands.

Practice Details: Inhale, engage right quadriceps and slowly extend right leg long, pressing through the mounds of right toes. Exhale, hinge knee and slowly lower foot down. Try to keep thigh parallel throughout exercise. If thigh does lower down, simply return to parallel after each repetition. After ten repetitions, bend knee and lower foot to floor. Repeat on other side.

Duration: 1-3 sets of 10 repetitions on each side.

Muscles Strengthened: Quadriceps

ON THE MAT RESTORATIVE POSES TOSTRETCH UPWARD FACING DOG

SUPPORTED SUPTA BADDHA KONASANA (SUPPORTED BOUND ANGLE POSE)

Starting Position: Sitting upright in Baddha Konasana (Bound Angle pose) draw the short side of bolster to sacrum.

Practice Details: Placing hands slightly behind you, on either side of bolster, slowly lower spine down. Feel Bolster is aligned perfectly along spinal column. Place hands comfortably either on belly, thighs or beside you with palms facing up.

Duration: Slow deep breaths in and out of nose as you completely relax for 5-10 minutes.

Muscles Stretched: Pectorals, Rectus Abdominus, Adductor Group, Tensor Fascia Lata

SUPPORTED SETU BANDHASANA (SUPPORTED BRIDGE POSE)

Starting Position: Lying on back with knees bent, feet hips width apart with heels as close as possible to buttocks.

Practice Details: Exhale, press down through the four corners of your feet Inhale, tuck tail, lift hips and peel spine off mat. Take a hold of block (low, medium or highest height depending on hip height preferred) and slide underneath your sacrum (wider across sacrum vs longer is best). Make sure to not place block underneath your lumbar curve…instead find the flatter part of your lower back closer to your tailbone.

Duration: Long slow deep breaths in and out of nose as you completely relax for 5-10 minutes.

Muscles Stretched: Pectorals, Rectus Abdominus, Illiopsoas, Quadriceps

OFF THE MAT TOOLS AND TECHNIQUES TO STRETCH UPWARD FACING DOG

WALL PECTORAL STRETCH

Starting Position: Stand facing wall. Spread arms out shoulder height into T position with palms facing wall.

Practice Details: Draw right forearm and hand up wall, perpendicular to floor. With left hand on hip, bring awareness into shoulders square over hips. Start to slowly turn to left with small steps. Maintain contact with right shoulder and wall. You may only be able to turn an inch or so. Listen to the wisdom of your right shoulder and chest area… respect your limitations and only go into a gentle stretch. Breathe deeply. When finished turn slowly back towards wall.

Duration: Hold stretch for 3-10 breaths on each side.

Muscles Stretched: Pectorals, Biceps

QUAD STRETCH

Starting Position: Stand facing wall. Place left hand lightly on wall to maintain balance.

Practice Details: Bend right knee and reach for outer ankle with right hand. Send tailbone towards floor, draw right knee slightly behind you and press right foot gently into right hand.

Duration: Hold stretch for 3-10 breaths on either leg.

Muscles Stretched: Iliopsoas, Quadriceps

DOWNWARD FACING DOG

Who am I?
Quieting down,
I journey within,
breath reaches out and
takes me by the hand,
into the depths I am lead,
finally, I find myself staring,
in amazed recognition,
at my own divinity.

-Jennilee

DOWNWARD FACING DOG

I take one more long, slow, deep inhale in Urdhva Mukha Svanasana, Upward Facing Dog, allowing my lungs to fill completely before allowing my exhale to initiate movement into Adho Mukha Svanasana, Downward Facing Dog. Pressing through spread fingers and palms, I activate my abdominal muscles to help flex my torso slightly, hinging and lifting my hips high in the air for this inverted "V" pose. Bending and straightening my knees, pedaling my heels, I explore any tension that has accumulated in my calves and hamstrings. Straightening my legs and spreading my toes wide I press my heels a little closer to the floor. I look at my feet, to see if they are hips width apart, and then proceed to find a drishti point to focus my steady gaze upon. With heels pressing down and kneecaps lifting towards my hip creases, the engagement of my quadriceps encourage a soft letting go in my hamstrings. Now, my hips can lift ever so slightly higher in the air.

Continuing to scan my body for ease in the pose, I spread my fingers wider, making sure I am continuously leaving full handprint impressions on my mat that are shoulders width apart. I broaden my shoulders as I spread my shoulder blades like wings from spine to outer ribs. A little puff of air into the kidney region of my mid to lower back ensures I am not compressing my spine into a backbend. I listen to my breath as I meditate here.

I wait for the next inspiration to guide me on my toes with hips held high, exhaling to slightly bend knees in order to float to the top of my mat. Inhaling, I lengthen and lift my spine, gazing at a still point in front of my toes. Exhaling, I fold into a much deeper forward fold. From the soles of my feet I can feel energy rise as I inhale to stand and sweep my arms over my head. With hands meeting above, I exhale to draw the downward current of energy into my heart. Pausing with hands at heart center I close my eyes and meditate on all the people, places, and experiences I am grateful for. Namaste.

Adho Mukha Svanasana

Adho - Downward   **Mukha** - Facing
Svana - Dog   **Asana** - Pose

Muscles Stretched
Muscles Strengthened

Downward Facing Dog Prep Pose
Child's Pose

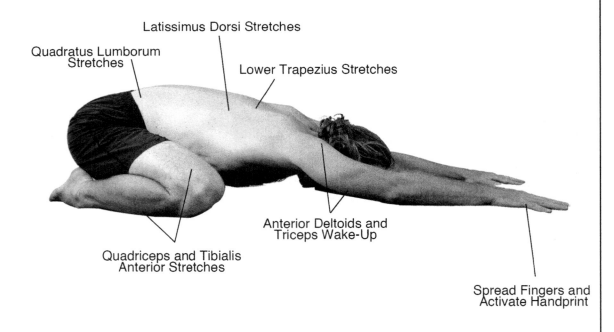

Latissimus Dorsi Stretches

Quadratus Lumborum
Stretches

Lower Trapezius Stretches

Anterior Deltoids and
Triceps Wake-Up

Quadriceps and Tibialis
Anterior Stretches

Spread Fingers and
Activate Handprint

Downward Facing Dog

Hips High

Lengthen Lower Back

Wide V of the Back
(Spreading Shoulder Blades)

Shoulders Away
from Ears

Neck Relaxed
and Long, Gaze
Between Heels

Quadriceps Active

Abdominals Active
(On Exhales Activate
Uddiyana Bandha)

Lower Heels,
Spread Toes

Spread Fingers,
Full Handprints

SIGNS OF IMBALANCE

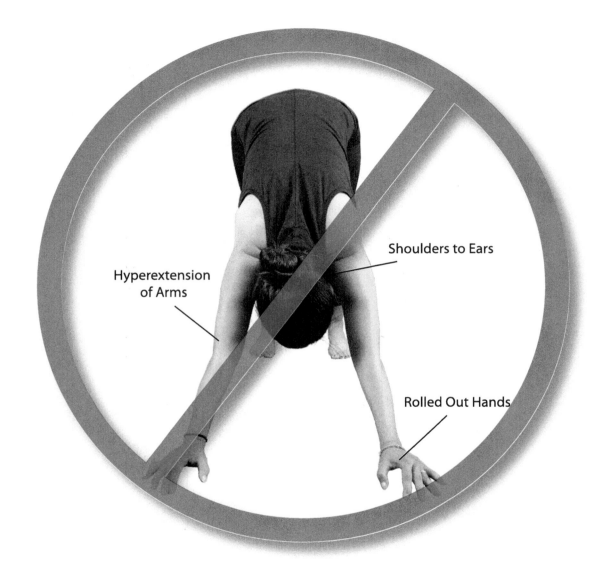

Hyperextension of Arms

Shoulders to Ears

Rolled Out Hands

Muscles to Strengthen

- Biceps
- Pectorals
- Subscapularis
- Lower Trapezius
- Abdominals

Muscles to Stretch

- Triceps
- Infraspinatus
- Levator Scapula
- Upper Trapezius

SIGNS OF IMBALANCE

Hanging on
Shoulders

Deep Hinge
at Hips

Shoulders
to Ears

Knees Bent

Muscles to Strengthen

- Pectorals
- Serratus Anterior
- Infraspinatus
- Lower Trapezius
- Quadratus Lumborum
- Gluteus Maximus
- Quadriceps

Muscles to Stretch

- Rhomboids
- Subscapularis
- Upper / MidTrapezius
- Subscapularis
- Iliopsoas
- Hamstrings
- Gastronecmius
- Soleus

ON THE MAT TOOLS AND TECHNIQUES TO STRENGTHEN DOWNWARD FACING DOG

NAVASANA (BOAT POSE)

Starting Pose: Sit on floor with knees bent. If uncomfortable to sit perched on sittingbones, tuck tail slightly and sit more on the sacrum. Place a block between thighs close to knees. Arms are parallel to the floor. Roll shoulders away from ears. Spread fingers wide. Keep neck long and chin parallel to the floor.

Practice Details: Inhale, find your balance by coming onto your toes first. Exhale, engage your abdominal muscles (draw navel towards spine) and slowly lift toes off floor bringing your lower legs parallel to the mat. Activate inner thighs as you gently squeeze thighs towards block. Feel free to straighten legs.

Duration: Hold pose for 3-10 long, deep exhales.

Muscles Strengthened: Abdominals, Iliopsoas, Quadriceps, Adductors, Anterior Deltoids

DOLPHIN PUSH-UPS

Starting Position: From tabletop position lower down on your forearms and interlace your fingers, elbows directly below your shoulders. Keeping feet hips width apart curl your toes under, press through the mounds of your toes and lift knees off mat into dolphin pose. Pressing through forearms, broadening across your shoulders, make sure you keep your neck long.

Practice Details: Inhale, shift forward to forearm plank, making sure to keep shoulders directly over elbows. Exhale navel to spine and press back to dolphin pose. Work with your breath and strength to flow from forearm plank to dolphin pose and back again. DO NOT USE MOMENTUM...tendency to go forward of elbows in forearm plank due to momentum can cause discomfort in elbows.

Duration: 1-3 sets of 10 repetitions.

Muscles Strengthened: Pectorals, Deltoids, Abdominals, Rectus Abdominus

OFF THE MAT TOOLS AND TECHNIQUES TO STRENGTHEN YOUR DOWNFACING DOG

BALL SQUEEZES

Starting Position: Seated or Standing. Take a hold of light weight ball. Hold with palm up. Keep elbow slightly bent.

Practice Details: Inhale, squeeze ball with 5-10% of strength. Hold for 1-3 seconds and then exhale, release grip. Repeat.

Duration: 1-3 sets of 10 repetitions.

Muscles Strengthened: Extrinsic Muscles of the hand, Flexor and Extensor Muscles of Forearm

OVERHEAD PRESS

Starting Position: Either seated or standing with knees bent. Draw two 1-5lb weights into chest (one in either hand). Open arms out to side, hinging elbows to a 90 degree angle, palms facing forward.

Practice Details: Inhale, slowly lift weights towards ceiling and gently touch them together. Exhale, slowly lower weights back to starting position of 90 degree angle. After ten repetitions, draw weights back to chest before lowering down.

Duration: 1-3 sets of 10 repetitions.

Muscles strengthened: Upper Trapezius, Lateral Deltoids

141

ON THE MAT TOOLS AND TECHNIQUES TO STRETCH YOUR DOWNWARD FACING DOG

HAMSTRING STRETCHES WITH STRAP

Starting Position: Lie on back with knees bent and feet on floor hips width apart.

Practice details: Draw right knee into chest, flex ankle and wrap strap under mounds of right toes. Hold equal lengths of strap tails in both hands. Inhale, straighten right leg to your comfortable range of motion. Exhale, bend knee. When finished, return to bent knee and release strap safely.

Duration: 10 repetitions each leg, range of motion naturally increasing each rep.

Muscles stretched: Hamstrings

PASCHIMOTTANASANA (INTENSE WEST STRETCH)

Starting Position: Sit on floor with legs stretched out in front of you and ankles flexed. If hamstrings are tight, bend knees as much as needed.

Practice Details: Inhale, reach overhead. Exhale, hinge at hips and reach towards front of mat space. Feel free to put hands on thighs for support or use a strap around mounds of feet. Depending on range of motion you may only be able to move torso to a 30-45% angle. Increased range of motion, hinge further and reach for toes. Always exhale to relax deeper into stretch. When finished, inhale back to starting position.

Duration: Dynamic – 10 inhales to lengthen, 10 exhales to hinge. Passive – Hold stretch for 3-10 breaths.

Muscles Stretched: Hamstrings,Gastrocnemius, Soleus Lower Back, Latissimus Dorsi (if reaching for toes)

OFF THE MAT TOOLS AND TECHNIQUES TO STRETCH DOWNWARD FACING DOG

CALF STRETCHES WITH BLOCK

Starting Position: Stand in front of a block placed firmly against wall in its lowest position. Hold onto wall for balance.

Practice Details: Place the mounds of your right toes on block. Keep heel on floor. Stay here and assess your calf tension. If you can stretch a little more, inhale and slowly lift the heel of your left foot, gently leaning body towards wall. Exhale, return left heel to floor and back away from the wall lean. When finished, slowly remove right foot from block. Rotate ankle before going to other side.

Duration: 1-3 sets of 10 repetitions.

Muscles Stretched: Soleus, Gastrocnemius

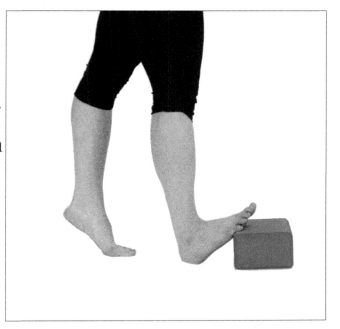

L SHAPE

Starting Position: Stand facing a chair placed firmly against a wall. Place both hands on back of chair.

Practice Details: Exhale, hinge at your hips and walk feet back from the chair. Make your way into a L shape position, hands on back of chair, arms in line with ears, abdominals supporting straightened spine, hips over feet. Bend knees if needefor hamstrings or lower back muscles. With each exhale, draw navel to spine, engaging abdominal muscles.

Duration: 1-3 sets of 10 long, slow, deep breaths.

Muscles Stretched: Hamstrings, Gastrocnemius, Soleus, Erector Spinae, Quadratus Lomborum, Pectorals, Latissimus Dorsi, Lower Trapesius

THE PERFECT CHATURANGA VINYASA FLOW

Try not to think

your movements

into being.

Instead, BREATHE

your movements

into being.

-Jennilee

Centering on Breath

Find a comfortable cross-legged seat in Sukhasana (sweet easy pose), lengthening spine as you root down through your sitting bones. Bring your awareness to your breath as it passes in and out through your nostrils. Feel your breath travelling up and down your nasal passageways. Hear your Ujjayi breath (victorious breath) swirling at the back of your throat. Notice your body responding to breath - upper chest rising and falling, ribs widening and narrowing, and your belly expanding and contracting. Focus on a nice even breath: same count in, same count out.

Half Neck Roll

On your next exhale, lower your chin towards your chest. Inhale right ear towards your right shoulder, exhale chin towards chest. Inhale left ear towards left shoulder, exhale chin towards chest. Continue to gently move your head from shoulder to shoulder in half circles, allowing your breath to support your movement. Go as slow as you can in order to release any tension in your neck. To finish, exhale chin to chest and inhale lift head into a neutral position.

Neck & Shoulder Stretches

Continue to sit with an upright spine. Exhale and allow your right ear to fall gently towards right shoulder. Lengthen out the left side of your neck. Walk your left fingertips out to the side of your mat. Breathe into any sensation you're feeling. Float your fingertips into the air and begin to explore your shoulder and neck as you make circles, arcs or figure eights with your arm. Be with your breath as you move. Inhale, return to center, both hands on your knees, looking ahead with neck in neutral position. Roll shoulders up back and down. Repeat on other side.

Seated Cat/Cow, add arms

With hands on your knees begin to flex and extend your spine. Inhale, start at your tail-bone and work your way up your spine towards the crown of your head, lifting ribs and eyes towards ceiling. Exhale, start at the crown of your head and spill down towards your tail, drawing your navel to spine as your round forward. Continue at your own pace, allowing your ujjayi breath to support and initiate the stretching and strengthening of spine and supporting muscles. After a few rounds, add your arms to the movement. Inhaling arms out wide, 90 degrees at elbows, spread fingers and palms facing front, opening across chest. Exhaling elbows and palms touch in front of you (elbows at heart level) opening across the back of the heart. Allow breath to support both movements. When finished, exhale return to center, elbows at 90 degrees, touching in front of heart center.

Pectoral Wake-Up

Change the crossing of your legs to the non-dominate cross. Inhale, lift arms forward and up to shoulder height. Bend elbows to 90 degrees and turns palms to face one another. Internally rotate your right humerus (upper arm bone) and place your right palm against inside of left elbow. Maintain 90 degree angles in both elbows. Exhale, lower shoulders away from ears. With 5-10% of your strength press your right hand into your left elbow at the same time you press your left elbow into your right hand. Hold for 10-30 seconds to engage pectoral (chest) muscles and then release. After three times, exhale and release arms into lap.

Seated Shoulder Vinyasa

Interlace hands in front of your heart. Exhale, send interlaced fingers and palms towards the front of your mat as you engage your abdominals and round your spine, tucking chin towards chest. Inhale, start with your tailbone, stack and straighten your spine, sending your interlaced fingers and palms towards ceiling. Exhale, release fingers and float arms down by the sides of your torso, interlacing fingers behind your lower back. Inhale, touch knuckles to floor behind your tail, squeeze shoulder blades together to lift your ribs and expand your heart. Gaze at the ceiling. Exhale, engage your abdominals and round forward into your lap, sending your interlaced fingers towards the ceiling. Lower interlaced fingers to lower back as you inhale to stack and straighten spine. Start flow from the top and continue to move with breath for a few rounds. To finish, release hands back to knees as you stack and straighten spine.

Amy's Shoulder & Chest Strengthening

Inhale, lift arms forward and up to shoulder height. Bend elbows to 90 degrees and press palms, wrists, forearms and elbows together. Try to keep shoulders away from ears as you encourage movement from upper arms to elbows to fingertips. Inhale lift arms up midline 1-6 inches. Exhale to lower. Inhale to lift arms 45 degrees over to right (external rotation of right upper arm and external rotation of left upper arm). Exhale to lower. Inhale lift arms up midline and exhale to lower. Inhale lift arms up 45 degrees to left and exhale to lower. Repeat the pattern a 5-10 times: center, right, center, left, center. Feel free to pick up the pace. When finished, return to center, exhale lower arms back to lap. Shoulder roll up, back and down.

Shoulder Stretches with a Strap

Take a moment to roll shoulders up, back and down a few times. Creating a wide "V" in front of you with your arms, take a hold of your strap with one end in either hand. Keeping wrists straight, inhale strap above your head (maintaining wide "V") and exhale the strap behind you (widen strap if you need to). Inhale strap overhead and exhale strap down in front of you. Continue moving from front to back and back to front, always allowing your breath to initiate and support your movement. Make sure to keep your arms and wrists straight. To finish, return to center, lower arms and place strap to the side. Take a moment to rotate your wrists.

Reverse Tabletop

Uncross your legs. Keeping your knees bent, plant your feet hips width apart. Place hands four to six inches behind your hips with fingertips towards front of mat space. Press through the four corners of your feet (mounds of big toes and small toes, and both sides of your heels) encouraging your toes to be happy and free. Exhale, engage lower abdominal muscles and slightly tuck your tail bone under, initiating the lift of your buttocks off the mat. Use your back body strength to lift your hips as high as your shoulders and knees. Gaze forward towards the front of your mat or straighten your neck and look straight above you. Shoulder blades glide towards each other underneath you, supporting the lifting and opening of your chest area. Exhale to release, lowering hips to the floor. Cross your ankles and roll over onto all fours.

Cat/Cow

Find yourself in a neutral tabletop position by bone stacking your shoulders and elbows over your wrists and stacking your hips directly over your knees. Inhale tailbone skyward, dip belly and lower ribs, lift heart, throat, chin and gaze upward (cow pose). Exhale, tuck your tailbone, engage abdominals to round spine, drawing your chin towards your chest and gaze at your navel (cat pose). Go at your own pace, allowing your breath to move and articulate your spine. Inhale to expand and open the front of your body, exhale to round and open the back of your body. Inhale to activate and strengthen the muscles of the back, exhale to activate and strengthen the muscles of the abdominal region. Inhale return to a neutral tabletop position.

C-Curve Spine Movement

Remain in your neutral flat table top position for the next two movements of your spine. Inhale encouraging a long neutral spinal column. Exhale, turn your head right to look past your shoulder at your right hip, shifting your left side ribs to the left, creating a c-curve with your spine. Inhale return to neutral flat tabletop position. Next exhale, turn your head to look past left shoulder at your left hip, shifting your right side ribs to the left, creating a c-curve with your spine. Inhale back to neutral position. Let your breath support you as move your spine laterally from side to side, creating space and length in the side body. Once finished, inhale to center.

Threading the Needle

Remain in your flat table top position for the last two movements of the spine. Walk your hands closer together, allowing your thumbs to touch underneath your sternum (chest bone). Pressing into your full right handprint, inhale look at your left hand as you peel it off the mat and reach it skyward, encouraging a torso rotation to the left. Maintain length in your spine as you reach high. Looking over your left shoulder at your hand, rotate your wrist and wiggle your fingers. Pause and spread your fingers wide, reaching your arms and hand a little higher. Exhale, thread your arm underneath your right armpit, through "the eye of your needle", engaging your obliques (abdominal muscles that help rotate the ribs around the spine), hovering your left shoulder, arm and hand off the mat. Inhale to unwind and reach for the ceiling. Repeat 5 times, strengthening muscles that help the spine in rotation. Exhale to return back to neutral tabletop position. Repeat whole sequence on the right side.

Wrist Stretch I

From flat tabletop position, begin to rotate one hand at a time, re-positioning hand so your fingertips are towards your knees. The next time your right fingertips are heading towards your right knee (left fingertips are forward) pause and then lean hips and shoulders back slightly towards your heels. Maintain contact between floor and heel of your right hand. Continuously draw shoulder back into its socket. To release, shift body forward to tabletop, release right hand and give it a gentle shake. Return to tabletop and begin sequence now on the left.

Wrist Stretch II

From flat tabletop position, begin to turn one hand over at a time, top of hand on mat, fingertips heading towards knees. Make sure to only do one hand at a time…always returning it back to neutral position before turning over the other hand. The next time your right hand is turned over, pause and then shift your hips and shoulders back towards heels. Maintain contact between floor and your carpal (wrist) bones. Continuously draw shoulder back into its socket. To release, shift body forward to tabletop, release right hand and give it a little shake. Return to tabletop and begin sequence now on the left.

Dolphin

From tabletop position lower down on your forearms and interlace your fingers, elbows directly below your shoulders. Keeping feet hips width apart curl your toes under, press through the mounds of your toes and lift knees off mat into dolphin pose. Pressing through forearms, broadening across your shoulders, make sure you keep your neck long. Bend and straighten your knees, lowering one heel at a time or both together towards the mat, exploring the muscles of your calves and hamstrings. Pause in stillness with your hips high in the air.

Forearm plank

From dolphin, exhale to engage your abdominals, gaze forward and lower your hips to hover parallel over the mat. You may need to wiggle or step your feet back to encourage a long line of energy between crown, shoulders, hips and heels. Gazing at your knuckles with a long neck, scan your body for proper alignment. Muscles of the shins, thighs, abdominals and chest are actively engaged to promote a steady lift as you hover across your mat. Feel free to lower on to knees if you tire, feel a lack of core strength or if sagging occurs, make sure to maintain a long line from knees to crown if this option is taken. Each exhale, engage your abdominal muscles, drawing navel upward towards spine to stabilize and support.

Dolphin Push-ups

From forearm plank, make sure to keep your elbows underneath your shoulders at all times, exhale press down through your forearms, engage your abdominals for support as you lift your hips high into dolphin pose. From dolphin pose, inhale forward to forearm plank, making sure to keep shoulders directly over elbows. Work with your breath and strength to flow from forearm plank to dolphin pose and back again. DO NOT USE MOMENTUM; the tendency to go forward of elbows in forearm plank due to momentum can cause discomfort in elbows. Finish in forearm plank. Lower on your knees and relax back into child's pose.

Balasana - Childs Pose

Knees apart, big toes touching, hinge at your hips and reach for the front of your mat space. From temple to temple rock your head from side to side. If your head does not touch the floor feel free to draw stacked fists underneath your forehead. Allow your belly to expand and contract as you breathe deeply. Child's pose is a pose of rest...please feel free to come to this pose at any time in your practice, grounding, balancing and resetting your energy in order to rejoin the practice refreshed and rejuvenated.

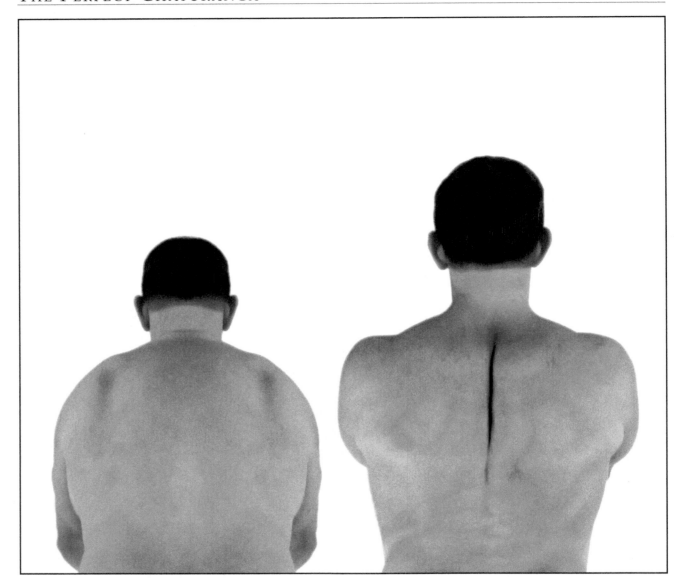

Rhomboid & Serratus Strengthening

Inhaling onto all fours, lower onto forearms, stepping feet back to forearm plank. This time bring awareness, activation and strength into your rhomboid muscles (between shoulder blades) and serratus anterior muscles (underneath shoulder blades attaching to side ribs). Make sure you are engaging front body muscles to support yourself in forearm plank. Feel free to lower onto your knees as before. Next inhale, allow your rhomboid muscles to draw your shoulder blades together (known as retraction). Next exhale, allow your serratus anterior muscles to draw your shoulder blades apart (protraction) and down onto your ribs. Slowly with your breath, move between the rhomboids working/strengthening and the serratus anterior muscles working/strengthening. Pause in neutral position, lower knees to the floor and come to child's pose variation.

Child's Pose (variation)

For this variation, keep knees and hands together as you hinge forward, hips towards heels. Feel free to sweep hands behind you, palms up, to frame feet, ankles or calves. If more comfortable, return to the variation of stacking fists underneath forehead. Whatever variation you take, make sure to encourage long, slow, deep breaths in and out of your nose.

Adho Mukha Svanasana - Downdog

From child's pose, inhale onto all fours (tabletop position) and press back into downward facing dog. Spread your fingers, pressing full handprints (pads, joints and palms) into the mat shoulders width apart. Draw shoulders away from ears as you roll your shoulder blades from spine to ribs, expanding and broadening across your upper back. Lengthen your spine as you lift your hips higher in this inverted "V" pose. Make sure to create space between your ribs and hips. Feel free to keep knees bent if needed. Otherwise, begin to straighten legs by engaging your quadriceps (kneecaps will lift towards hip crease). Spread your toes wide, feet hips width apart, heels reaching for the floor (may not touch). Relax your head, gazing at a still point between your feet or legs. Long, slow deep breaths.

Plank

On your next inhale, shift forward to plank pose. Take a moment to bone-stack your shoulders, elbows and wrists. Maintain spread fingers and full hand activation. Your energy is head forward and heels back. Feel your heels high over your spread toes. The muscles on the front of your body are actively holding up your bones: shins, knees, thighs, abs, and chest. Make sure your shoulders are drawn away from your ears and your shoulder blades are spread and flattened on top of your posterior (back) ribs. Find a still point to gaze about an inch in front of your fingers. This will ensure you keep your heart lifted and buoyant. Each exhale engage your abdominals, drawing your navel up towards your spine, strengthening your core.

Pushups

From plank, gentle lower knees to the floor. Make sure you are now one long line from knees to crown of head. Continue to engage your abdominals to strengthen and support spine. Maintain your gaze a few inches in front of your fingertips, preventing a collapse in your chest/heart area. Encouraging your breath to support your movement inhale to lower your torso to the floor, exhale to engage abdominals and press your torso away from the floor. Make sure to brush your ribs with your elbows both on the way down and the way up, as if elastic bands were connecting them. After ten push-ups, lie down on mat with your arms by your sides.

Salabasana – Locust Pose

   With your forehead on the mat, extend your arms down by your sides with your palms facing the ceiling. Legs are hips width apart behind you or you can bring them to touch. Inhale, gaze forward, lift your upper body off the mat, keeping arms and hands on mat. Exhale lower down. Next inhale, lift both upper body and legs off the mat. Exhale lower down. Final inhale lift upper body, lower body and your arms, even interlace hands behind you as you draw shoulder blades towards each other (hold onto a strap behind your back if you cannot interlace fingers). Exhale to lower down, releasing your head to the right for a few breaths.

Ardha Dhanurasana – Half Floor Bow

Inhale and return to a neutral neck, forehead on the mat. On your next inhale, extend your left arm towards the front of the room and reach your left leg long behind you with pointed toes. Exhale, bend right knee and reach back for right ankle, thumb towards floor. On an inhale, lift upper and lower body off the mat. Left side of the body your focus is on length and strength. Right side of your body, focus is on strengthening the back body and stretching the front as you back bend. Inhale to lift a little higher off the mat. Exhale to lower and switch sides. After both sides are finished, lie down and turn head to the left for a few long slow deep breaths. With a neutral neck, inhale press up to tabletop and exhale back into downward facing dog.

Ragdoll

From downward facing dog, look forward and walk until your toes meet the heels of your hands. Slightly bend your knees, relax your torso over your thighs and tuck your thumbs into opposite elbow creases. Exhale and explore your foundation: the four corners of each foot (mound of big toe, mound of pinkie/baby toe and both sides of your heel). Sway around these four corners, allowing gravity and deep breathes to help you out as you relax your upper body onto your strong lower body. Slow down and still your movement, keeping knees in a soft bend as you slightly tuck your tail. Inhaling, roll up slowly, stacking all the bones in your body in. Keeping your arms by your sides, your head will be the last thing to stack. Inhale shoulders up towards your ears and exhale them back and down.

Tadasana – Mountain Pose

Maintain your feet hips width apart. Exhale and root down through the four corners of each foot. Pick up your toes, spread them, and then place them back down one at a time. Never clench your toes in yoga – always keep them happy and free of tension. Inhale, scan your body from feet towards head, drawing energy up through your ankles, knees and hips. Allow the muscles of your upper and lower legs to isometrically contract, hugging and stabilizing your bones. Exhale, your tailbone is heavy toward the floor and your lower abdominal muscles are active. Feel your next inhale travel up the natural curves of your spinal column to the crown of your head. Lower your chin just slightly to lengthen the back of your neck. Shoulders down your back, exhale into your elbows, wrists, hands and extended fingers. Keep your palms facing your thighs. Find a place in front of you to softly gaze at. Listen to your breath.

Sun salutation A with Cobra/Anjeeneyasana

1. Step feet together, samasthiti (equal standing stillness pose,) with hands at heart center
2. Inhale, hook thumbs and extend arms overhead, stretching whole body.
3. Exhale, hands through heart center as you hinge to uttanasana, standing forward fold.
4. Inhale, extend and lift your spine into ardha uttanasana, half way lift.
5. Exhale, plant hands and step right foot back, right knee down.
6. Inhale arms overhead into Ajaneeyasana, pose of devotion.
7. Exhale step back to plank, knees down, lower body down.
8. Inhale upper body off mat into bhujangasana, cobra pose.
9. Exhale lower down and press back into downward facing dog.
10. Inhale step right foot forward, lower left knee and lift arms overhead, Anjaneeyasana.
11. Exhale step forward, fold forward uttanasana
12. Inhale, extend and lift your spine into ardha uttanasana, half way lift.
13. Exhale, fold deeper into uttanasana
14. Inhale, hook thumbs and extend arms over head.
15. Exhale samasthiti, hands home to heart.

REPEAT WHOLE SEQUENCE ON LEFT SIDE

Garudasana – Eagle Pose

From Samasthiti (Stillness Pose), inhale and extend arms out to "T" position. With soft knees, exhale, hook your right elbow underneath your left elbow, wrapping your right forearm around your left forearm. Either interlace your fingers or staggered prayer position. Bending your knees as if sitting in a chair, exhale ground through the four corners of your left foot and inhale lift right leg, wrapping right thigh over left, hooking right toes around left calf if possible. Sitting low in your imaginary chair, allow tail to hang heavy as you engage lower abdominal muscles to support lower back, lifting ribs off of hips and drawing shoulders down away from your ears. Send elbows forward to stretch between shoulder blades and lift elbows to the height of your shoulders. Find a spot to stare at in front of you somewhere as you calmly breathe. Inhale to release, slowly unwinding all your limbs. Return to your stillness pose before other side.

*some yoga systems teach leg placement first followed by arm placement.

Sun Salutation B with Chaturanga/Updog

1. Step feet together, Samasthiti (equal standing stillness pose,) with hands at heart center
2. Bend knees as if to sit in a chair, inhaling arms over head in wide "v", utkatasana
3. Exhale hands through heart center, fold and straighten your legs into uttanasana
4. Inhale, half lift spine and gaze at a drishti spot in front of toes, ardha uttanasana
5. Maintaining your drishti, step/float back to chaturanga dandasana
6. Inhale, toes propel you forward to urdhva mukha svanasana. Straighten and stack the bones of your arms, expand your chest and keep thighs and knees off the mat
7. Exhale, press mat away, hinge at hips and roll over toes into adho muhka svanasana
8. Inhale right foot forward to Warrior I. Exhale chaturanga, inhale upward facing dog, exhale downward facing dog.
9. Inhale left foot forward to Warrior I. Exhale chaturanga, inhale upward facing dog, exhale downward facing dog. 5 breaths in downdog.
10. Exhale all breath out and float to top of mat.
11. Inhale, half lift spine and gaze at a drishti spot in front of toes, ardha uttanasana
12. Exhale fold deeper into uttanasana
13. Inhale utkatasana, fierce pose.
14. Exhale samasthiti, hands home to heart.

Natarajasana – Dancer's Pose

From Samasthiti, place your left hand on your hip as you exhale ground down through the four corners of your left foot. With your right elbow bent 90 degrees at elbow, hand extended out to the side, inhale bend your right knee and take a hold of either your outer ankle/foot (thumb down) or your inner foot/arch (thumb up). Draw your knees closer together, your hips are squared towards the front of your mat space. Inhale and extend your left arm overhead. Find the bow you practiced earlier on the floor, pressing your right foot into your right hand. On your next exhale, maintaining the back bend, hinge forward on your left thigh, extending left arm out in front of you. Your drishti is your left thumb, don't allow your arm/hand to dip lower than your browline to keep your heart lifted and buoyant in your chest. To release, inhale upright, right arm up, back and down. Return to Samasthiti before practicing on the other side.

Flow to the Floor

1. Step feet together, Samasthiti (equal standing stillness pose,) with hands at heart center

2. Inhale, sweep arms out and extend arms overhead, stretching whole body.

3. Exhale, open arms, draw shoulder blades together, swan dive down, hinging into uttanasana (standing forward fold).

4. Inhale, extend and lift your spine into ardha uttanasana (half way lift).

5. Exhale, plant hands and step back to high-low plank or float back to low plank chaturanga.

6. Inhale, toes propel you forward to upward facing dog.

7. Exhale, press back into downward facing dog

8. Inhale, shift forward to high plank.

9. Exhale, knees down.

10. Lower body down to floor.

Dhanurasana - Floor bow

Forehead on the floor, neck in neutral position, inhale bend both knees and reach back for outer ankles, thumbs towards floor. If you cannot reach both ankles, wrap strap around ankles and reach for strap. Exhale, feel your lower ribs, lower belly and pubic bones root down into mat. On an inhale, both upper and lower body will lift off the mat. Keep your neck long, squeeze shoulder blades together and press feet into your hands. Back body strength will encourage a more expansive opening in the front body. Each inhale, lift your body higher and higher off the mat. Exhale to lower down, create pillow for your forehead, windshield wipe your lower legs side to side. Neutral position, extend legs behind you, press back into down dog.

Ustrasana – Camel Pose

From downward facing dog, lower your knees hips width apart onto mat. Walk your hands back towards body and roll up to stand on your knees. Curl your toes under so that your heels are stacked over toes. Place your hands on your lower back with finger tips towards your tail. Feel the support of your hands. On an inhale, lift your ribs, chest and gaze towards the ceiling. As if a small ball or a piece of round fruit were placed between your chin and your chest, keep your neck long and lifted. Stay here unless it is in your practice to reach simultaneously for both heels with your hands, deepening your heart opening posture. Only if you have a healthy neck would you let your head tilt back, gaze to back wall. Any neck vulnerability, keep your chin on that imaginary ball/round piece of fruit on your chest. To come out of this pose, inhale return hands to lower back and stack spine back to neutral. Sit on heels in a kneeling meditation pose. Encourage long, slow deep breathes in and out of your nose.

Gomukhasana – Cow-Facing Pose with Fold Forward

Hinge forward and make your way to flat tabletop position. Place your right knee behind your left knee and sweep your feet to the sides of your mat. Sit your buttocks between your heels (you may need to sit on a block or blanket). Your right knee will be stacked directly over the left in time. Try not to sit on your feet. With an upright spine exhale and let your hips release tension. On an inhale, sweep arms out to "T" position. Left arm reaches over head and as you bend at the left elbow give yourself a pat on the back. Rotate your right wrist with thumb towards the floor, hinge your right elbow joint and draw your hand behind you, palm facing away from back. Eventually, as shoulders release of tension, fingers will hook together in a ganesha grip between your shoulder blades. You may need a strap to help get the fingers closer together. Maintain an upright spine, drawing elbows closer towards the body. For a deeper stretch, maintain the bind of hands and exhale to hinge and fold forward. Stay here for a few long, slow, deep breaths. To release, inhale back to neutral spine. Exhale to windmill the arms back to your sides, hands on resting on your knees. Return to neutral tabletop before other side.

Ardha Matsyendrasana – Half Lord of the Fishes

From neutral tabletop position, cross your ankles and roll back to take a seat. With your left knee bent towards front of your mat space, left outer thigh touching the floor, take your right foot over left thigh and step it on the mat, right ankle touching outer edge of your left knee (option to keep your left leg straight if any knee discomfort occurs). Place both hands on your right knee and lengthen your spine. With left arm hugging right knee place your tented right fingertips on the floor just behind your tailbone. Inhale to lengthen your spine and exhale to twist, gazing over your right shoulder. To go deeper, place left elbow (bent at 90 degree angle) on the outer edge of right knee, fingers spread wide. To deepen, guide the left hand to the left knee. Half bind, wrap right arm around lower back, reaching for left hip crease. Full bind is when left arm threads the eye of the needle and fingers hook together in a ganesha grip behind left hip. No matter what arm configuration you chose, always maintain the mantra: inhale lengthen spine, exhale twist. One more exhale to go deeper and then inhale to return to center. Change sides.

Tarasana - Star Pose

In a seated position draw the soles of your feet together. Gauge the distance between groin and heels by measuring with straight arms and palms together (where fingertips touch heels is a good distance). On an exhale, draw navel to spine and drape yourself over your legs, as if there were a big ball perched in that space. Hands can interlace around feet. If possible, weave a finger between each and every toe. Let your exhales relax you. If hanging your head towards your feet is uncomfortable in any way, place a block on your feet or behind the heels for your head to rest. This is meant to be a relaxing, restorative pose. Forward bending is relaxing for your nervous system. When it is time to move out of pose, inhale and slowly roll up one vertebra at a time.

Savasana – Corpse Pose

Turn around and lie down. It is now time to rest and aid the body in its quest to assimilate all the benefits attained by your effort and practice. Allow yourself to be as relaxed as possible. Place your legs a comfortable distance apart from each other, toes relaxed out to the sides of your mat. With your arms a comfortable distance from your body, have your palms face up, offering more ease across your chest and heart space. Allow your chin to relax a slight bit towards your throat encouraging the back of your neck to remain long. Close your eyes and relax the muscles of your face. As you scan your body with your breath, relax a little bit more with each exhale. Your exhales will always relax you. Rest here for at least 5 minutes. When it is time to move, roll to your right in fetal position and give yourself a hug. Honor yourself for practicing your yoga. The world is now a better place. Namaste.

ADVANCED CHATURANGA

Exhale all your

breath out.

Pause.

Engage.

Suspend.

Yes,

Fly, yogis, fly.

-Jennilee

ADVANCED CHATURANGA

Once the fundamentals of Chaturanga Dandasana are learned and mastered there is a choice to advance in your practice of this pose. Float back to chaturanga dandasana from ardha uttanasana (halflift), bakasana (crow/crane) or any of the other challenging arm balances is quite a fun, invigorating and empowering experience. Unfortunately, floating back to chaturanga incorrectly can lead to traumatic and/or repetitive motion injury. NEVER JUMP BACK TO HIGH PLANK – this jarring finish (landing with straight arms) can cause traumatic shoulder joint injury. Instead, with an air of grace and suppleness, FLOAT BACK TO LOW PLANK. Mastery and proper use of breath, bandhas, bone alignment, muscle activation and joint integration is a must if injury is to be avoided and safe, playful ease is to be experienced.

ROLLING OUT TO CHATURANGA

1. Inhale onto toes and roll out one vertebra at a time from tail to crown
2. As you roll through engage Mula & Uddiyana Bandhas
3. Exhale lower down into a perfect chaturanga dandasana

FLOATING INTO CHATURANGA FROM ARDHA UTTANASANA

1. Inhale ardha uttanasa – find drishti (focal point 6-12" in front of your toes)
2. Exhale press into hands, engage Mula & Uddiyana bandhas
3. With bandhas actively engaged and drishti maintained, float up and back
4. Softly land in a perfect chaturanga dandasana

FLOATING INTO CHATURANGA FROM BAKASANA

1. Inhale in Bakasana – find drishti (focal point 6-12" in front of your toes)
2. Exhale press into hands, engage Mula & Uddiyana bandhas
3. With bandhas actively engaged and drishti maintained, float up and back
4. Softly land in a perfect chaturanga dandasana

CONCLUSION

The light within me
honors
the light within
you.
When you are in
your place of pure
love and peace
and I am in mine...
We are one.

Namaste.

CONCLUSION

It is very exciting, this modern day yoga revolution! More and more people are trying out the ancient discipline of body-mind yoking. Studios are opening in every neighborhood, more and more classes are being offered in gyms, and when the weather is just right yoga is offered in almost every park in the world! In some studios there are upwards of ten new students a day trying out yoga. There are studios that have 40-60 people a class, 15 minutes between classes, 3-4 classes in a row…sometimes with only one teacher teaching all those people! Where once it was like pulling teeth to get people to try yoga (the oft quoted replies, "it's not for me," "too slow," and "I already stretch") now fast food billboards are showing people in yoga postures!

With this expansion, though, comes a huge responsibility from studio owners, yoga teachers and students alike. WE NEED TO OFFER AND PRACTICE SAFE, INTELLIGENTLY DESIGNED YOGA SEQUENCES! Studio owners: make sure your teachers are trained by a reputable teacher training, continuing their education with classes, workshops and further training, practicing self-care in order to support happy teaching (vs yoga teacher burn out) and offering safe & intelligent classes (take their classes!) Teachers: make sure you are doing the above things, even asking studio owners to subsidize your continuing education. Students: please take personal responsibility for the health and well-being of your own body. Make sure to attend appropriate physical fitness level classes! Always, always, ALWAYS listen to your bodies' wisdom…if your intuition says something is possibly injurius, then don't do it. Back gracefully out of the posture, go to the depth/ angle that feels good and right to you, and speak to the teacher after class. A genuinely great yoga teacher will always be ready, willing and able to help you, the student, learn more about what is right for your personal practice!

Let us practice yoga for the rest of our lives – and do it safely and intelligently! Over time, all practices of yoga will eventually lead us all home; home to both our individual and collective hearts. Mama Earth needs us, her children, to wake-up and start honoring and loving ourselves, each other, all her creatures, and so importantly, Mama Earth herself!

The very essence of yoga is such a sweet truth:
WE ARE ONE LOVE. Namaste.

APPENDIX A:
Language of the Asanas

Understanding without practice is better than practice without understanding.

Understanding with practice is better than understanding without practice.

Residing in your true nature is better than understanding or practice.

-Upanishads

Language of the Asanas

Sanskrit is the most ancient of the Indo-European languages (Sanskrit, Greek, and Latin). The names of asanas (yoga postures) can be categorized in four ways: human anatomy, animals, hindu sages & deities and objects (mostly found in nature). Additionally, names of poses usually include numbers and/or specific characteristics of the pose.

NUMBERS

1. Eka
2. Dwi
3. Tri
4. Chatur
5. Pancha
6. Shat
7. Sapta
8. Ashta
9. Nava
10. Dasha

ANATOMY

1. Anga: limb
2. Anghusta: big toe
3. Anguli: fingers
4. Bhuja: arm
5. Hasta: hand
6. Janu: knee
7. Jattara: stomach
8. Karna: ear
9. Mukha: face
10. Pada: foot/ leg
10. Prana: breath/ lifeforce
11. Sarvanga: whole body
12. Sirsa: head
13. Sava: corpse

ANIMALS

1. *Baka: crow*

2. *Bheka: frog*

3. *Bhujanga: cobra/ serpent*

4. *Go: cow*

5. *Kapota: pigeon/ dove*

6. *Krouncha: heron*

7. *Kurma: turtle*

8. *Marjaryi: cat*

9. *Matsya: fish*

10. *Sasanga: rabbit*

11. *Salabha: locust/ grasshopper*

12. *Svana: dog*

13. *Ustra: camel*

DEITIES/SAGES

1. Ganesha: Elephant God, remover (and placer) of obstacles, son of Shiva, accomplished yogi, lover of sweets.

2. Garuda: A mystical lion-eagle creature, the vehicle of Vishnu, God of Preservation. Also, national symbol of Indonesia. Discussed in Garuda Upanishad, Garuda Purana, and epic poem of India, the Mahabharata.

3. Hanuman: Incarnate of Shiva, Monkey God, devoted warrior servantt of the righteous King Rama (incarnate of Vishnu). In his heart contains the divine feminine and masculine as Sita and Ram.

4. Kali: Goddess of death, destruction and time. Shiva's counterpart. Seen with skulls around her neck and blood dripping from her tongue.

5. Matsyendra: Lord of the Fishes; when Shiva told Parvarti about yoga, a fish heard, learned and practiced. In his evolved state he has given us the gift of Shiva's yoga.

6. Marichi: son of Brahma, the god of creation and grandfather of Surya, the sun god.

7. Nataraja: Shiva as Cosmic Dancer. Shiva dances transformation into being.

8. Sage Vashista: One of the seven Great Rishis. The sage that told Rama the Truth of his divinity in the Yoga Vasistha.

9. Sage Vishvamitra: Said to be the revealer of the Gayatri Mantra, the most profound and powerful mantra ever uttered.

10. Virabhadra: Avenging his wife Sati's death, Lord Shiva cut off one of his dreadlock's and out sprang Shiva's fiercest warrior, Virabhadra (vira means "hero" and bhadra means "friend"). Virabhadra is said to have fought valiantly and effortlessly for his love of the divine feminine.

OBJECTS

1. *Asana: seat/ posture*

2. *Bala: child*

3. *Chandra: moon*

4. *Danda: rod/ staff*

5. *Dhanu: bow*

6. *Hala: plough*

7. *Mala: garland*

8. *Mudra: seal*

9. *Nava: boat*

10. *Padma: lotus*

11. *Parigha: gate*

12. *Setu: bridge*

14. *Tada: mountain*

15. *Tola: scales*

16. *Vajra: thunderbolt*

17. *Vira: hero*

18. *Vrksa: tree*

CHARACTERISTICS

1. Adho: downward
2. Ardha: half
3. Baddha: bound
4. Dukkha: stale, stagnant, negative
5. Kona: angle
6. Nirlamba: without support
7: Paschima: west direction
8. Paripurna: complete
9. Parivrtta: revolved
10. Parsva: side

11. Pida: pressure
12. Prasarita: spread out
13. Purva: east direction
14. Salamba: with support
15. Sthiti: stability
16. Sukkha: sweet, easy
17. Supta: reclining
18. Upavistha: seated
19. Uttana: intense stretch
20. Utthita: extended
21. Urdva: upward

APPENDIX B:

Yogi's Library

You are the Truth

from foot to brow.

Now,

What else would

you like to know?

-Rumi

YOGA PHILOSOPHY

Brunton, Paul. *The Hidden Teaching Beyond Yoga*. York Beach, ME: Samuel Weiser, 2d rev ed., 1984. First published 1941.

Brunton, Paul. *A Search in Secret India*. York Beach, ME: Samuel Weiser, rev. ed., 1985. First published 1935.

Chopra, Deepak. *The Seven Spiritual Laws of Yoga: A Practical Guide to Healing Body, Mind and Spirit*. Hoboken, NJ: John Wiley & Sons, Inc., 2004.

Easwaran, Eknath. *The Bhagavad Gita: A Classic of Indian Spirituality*. Berkeley, CA: Blue Mountain Center for Meditation, 2007.

Eliade, Mircea. *Yoga: Immortality and Freedom*. Princeton, NJ: Princeton University Press, 1973.

Eliade, Mircea. *Patanjali and Yoga*. New York, NY: Schocken Books, 1975.

Feurstein, Georg. *Introduction to the Bhgavad-Gita: Its Philosophy and Cultural Setting*. Wheaton, IL: Quest Books, 1983.

Feurstein, Georg. *The Philosophy of Classical Yoga*. Rochester, VT: Inner Traditions International, 1996.

Feurstein, Georg. *The Yoga Tradition: It's History, Literature, Philosophy and Practice*. Prescott, AZ: Hohm Press, 2001.

Feurstein, Georg. *The Yoga-Sutra of Patanjali: A New Translation and Commentary*. Rochester, VT: Inner Traditions International, 1989.

Frawley, David. *Yoga and Ayurveda: Self-Healing and Self-Realization*. Twin Lakes, WI: Lotus Press, 1999.

Frawley, David. *Yoga: The Greater Tradition*. San Rafael, CA: Mandala Publishing, 2008.

Freeman, Richard. *The Mirror of Yoga: Awakening the Intelligence of Body and Mind*. Boston, MA: Shambhala Publications, Inc. 2010.

Iyengar, BKS. *Light on the Yoga Sutras of Patanjali*. San Francisco, CA: HarperSanFrancisco, 1993.

YOGA PHILOSOPHY

Maehle, Gregor. *Yoga Meditation: Through Mantra, Chakras and Kundalini to Spiritual Freedom.* Crabbes Creek, Australia: Kaivalya Publications, 2013.

Mascaro, Juan and Anonymous. *The Upanishads.* Penguin Books. London, England: Penguin Books Ltd, 1965.

Muller, Max. *The Six Systems of Indian Philosophy.* London: Longmans, Green & Co., repr 1928.

Prabhavananda, Swami. *The Spiritual Heritage of India.* Hollywood, CA: Vedanta Press, 1979.

Prabhavananda, Swami and Isherwood, Christopher. *How To Know God: The Yoga Aphorisms of Patanjali.* Hollywood, CA: Vedanta Press, 1981.

Rama, Swami, Rudolf Ballentine, and Swami Ajaya. *Yoga and Psychotherapy: The Evolution of Consciusness.* Glenview, IL: Himalayan Institute, 1976.

Satchidananda, Swami. *The Yoga Sutras of Patanjali.* Virginia: Integral Yoga Publications, 1990.

Stone, Michael. *The Inner Tradition of Yoga.* Boston, MA: Shambhala Publications, Inc., 2008.

Svoboda, Robert E. *Aghora: At the Left Hand of God.* Albuquerque, NM: Brotherhood of Life, 1986.

Vivekananda, Swami. *The Complete Works of Swami Vivekananda.* Mayavati, India: Advaita Ashrama, 1947-1955. 8 vols.

Yogananda, Paramahansa. *Autobiography of a Yogi.* Los Angeles, CA: Self-Realization Fellowship, 1987. First Publ. 1946.

Yogananda, Paramahansa. *God Talks with Arjuna: The Bhagavad Gita – Royal Science of God-Realization.* Los Angeles, CA: Self-Realization Fellowship, 1995. 2 vols.

Zimmer, Heinrich. *Philosophies of India.* Edited by Joseph Campbell. New York, NY: Harper & Row, 1962.

Bailey, Alice. *Serving Humanity: A Compilation.* New York, NY: Lucis Publishing Company, 1987.

Baran, Josh. *The Tao of Now: Daily Wisdom from Mystics, Sages, Poets, and Saints.* Charlottesville, VA: Hampton Roads Publishing, 2008.

Bubba (Da) Free John. *The Enlightenment of the Whole Body.* Middletown, CA: Dawn Horse Press, 1978.

Campbell, Joseph. *The Power of Myth with Bill Moyers.* New York, NY: Anchor Books, 1991.

Campbell, Joseph and Osbon, Diane K. *Reflections on the Art of Living: A Joseph Campbell Companion.* New York, NY: HarperCollins Publishers, Inc., 1991

Chodron, Pema. *Start Where You Are: A Guide to Compassionate Living.* Boston, MA: Shambhala Publications, Inc., 1994.

Coelho, Paulo. *The Alchemist.* San Francisco, CA: HarperSanFrancisco, 1994.

Dass, Ram. *Be Here Now.* New York, NY: The Crown Publishing Group, 1978.

Dalai Lama, His Holiness. *The Art of Happiness, 10th Anniversary Edition: A Handbook for Living.* New York, NY: Penguin Group (USA), 1998.

Hanh, Thich Nhat. *You Are Here: Discovering the Magic of The Present Moment.* Boston, MA: Shambhala Publications, Inc., 2009.
Huxley, Aldous. *The Perennial Philosophy.* New York, NY: HarperCollins Publishers, 1945.

Judith, Anodea. *Eastern Body, Western Mind: Psychology and the Chakra System as a Path to the Self.* Berkely, CA: Celestial Arts, 1996.

Judith, Anodea. *Wheels of Light: A User's Guide to the Chakra System.* Woodbury, MN: Llewellyn Publications, 1999.

Jung, Carl Gustav. *Psychology of the East.* Princeton, NJ: Princeton University Press, 1978.

PERENNIAL PHILOSOPHY

Ladinsky, Daniel and Various. *Love Poems from God: Twelve Sacred Voices from the East and West.* New York, NY: Penguin Group, 2002.

Maslow, Abraham. *Towards a Psychology of Being.* Princeton, NJ: Van Nostrand, 1962.

Myss, Caroline, PhD. *Anatomy of the Spirit: The Seven Stages of Power and Healing.* New York, NY: Three Rives Press, 1996.

Nathwani, Ravi, and Vogt, Kate. *Mala of the Heart: 108 Sacred Poems.* Novato, CA: New World Library, 2010.

Nepo, Mark. *The Book of Awakening: Having the Life You Want by Being Present to the Life You Have.* SanFrancisco,CA: Conari Press, 2000.

Singer, Michael A. *The Untethered Soul: A Journey Beyond Yourself.* Oakland, CA: New Harbinger Publications, Inc., 2007.

Thurman, Robert. *Inner Revolution: Life, Liberty and the Pursuit of Real Happpiness.* New York, NY: The Berkeley Publishing Group, 1998.

Tolle, Ekhart. *A New Earth: Awakening to Your Life's Purpose.* New York, NY: Penguin Group(USA), 2005.

Trungpa, Chogyam. *Cutting Through Spiritual Materialism.* Boulder and London: Shambhala, 1973.

Trungpa, Chogyam. *Shambhala: The Sacred Path of the Warrior.* Boston, MA: Shambhala Publications, Inc., 1984.

Tweedie, Irina. *Daughter of fire: A Diary of a Spiritual Training with a Sufi Master.* Nevada City, CA: Blue Dolphin Publishing, 1986.

Wilber, Ken. *The Atman Project: A Transpersonal View of Human Development.* Wheaton, IL: Theosophical Publishing House, 1980.

Williamson, Marianne. *A Return to Love: Reflections on the Principles of A course In Miracles.* New York, NY: HarperCollins Publishers, 1992.

Aldous, Suzi Hately. *Anatomy and Asana: Preventing Yoga Injuries.* Calgary, CA: Functional Synergy Press, 2004.

Bachman, Nicolai. *The Language of Yoga: Complete A to Y Guide to Asana Names, Sanskrit Terms and Chants.* Boulder, CO: Sounds True, Inc., 2005.

Boccio, Frank Jude. *Mindfulness of Yoga: The Awakened Breath, Body, and Mind.* Boston, MA: Wisdom Publications, 2004.

Brown, Christina. *The Yoga Bible: The definitive Guide to Yoga Postures.* Hampshire, England: Godsfield Press, Ltd, 2003.

Calais-Germain, Blandine. *Anatomy of Movement.* Seattle, WA: Eastland Press, Inc., 2007.

Coulter, Daniel. *Anatomy of Hatha Yoga: A Manual for Students, Teachers and Practitioners.* Marlboro, VT: Body and Breath, Inc., 2001.

Desikachar, TKV. *The Heart of Yoga: Developing a Personal Practice.* Rochester, VT: Inner Traditions International, 1995.

Grilley, Paul. *Yin Yoga: Principles and Practice – 10th Anniversary Edition.* Ashland, OR: White Cloud Press, 2012.

Iyengar, BKS. *Light on Yoga: Yoga Dipika.* New York, NY: Schocken Books, 1966.

Iyengar, BKS. *Yoga: The Path to Holistic Health.* London, England: Dorling Kindersley Ltd, 2001.

Farhi, Donna. *Yoga Mind, Body and Spirit: A Return to Wholeness.* New York, NY: Holt Paperbacks, 2000.

Kaminoff, Leslie and Matthews, Amy. *Yoga Anatomy – 2ed.* Champaign, IL: Human Kinetics, 2012.

Kapit, Wynn and Elson, Lawrence M. *The Anatomy Coloring Book – 4ed.* Essex, England: Pearson Education Limited, 2014.

Kirk, Martin and Brook Boon, Daniel Dituro. *Hatha Yoga Illustrated: For Greater Strength, Flexibility and Focus.* Champaign, IL: Human Kinethics, 2003.

ANATOMY & ASANA

Kraftsow, Gary. *Yoga and Wellness: Ancient Insights for Modern Healing.* New York, NY: Penguin,.

Lasseter, Judith Hanson, PhD, PT. *Yogabody: Anatomy, Kiniesology, and Asana.* Berkeley, CA: Rodmell Press, 2009.

LePage, Joseph and Lillian. *The Yoga Teachers Toolbox: Yoga Posture Cards for Integrating Body, Mind and Spirit.* Garretsville, OH: Integrative Yoga Therapy, 2005.

Long, Ray, MD, FRCSC. *The Key Muscles of Yoga: Scientific Key, Vol I.* Bandha Yoga Publications, 2006.

Long, Ray, MD, FRCSC. *The Key Poses of Hatha Yoga: Scientific Keys, Vol II.* Bandha Yoga Publications, 2009.

Maehle, Gregor. *Ashtanga Yoga: Practice and Philosophy.* Novato, CA: New World Library, 2006.

Macgregor, Kino. *The Power of Ashtanga Yoga: Developing a Practice That Will Bring You Strength, Flexibility & Inner Peace.* Boston, MA: Shambhala Publications, 2013.

McCall, Timothy, MA and Yoga Journal. *Yoga as Medicine: The Yogic Prescription for Health and Healing.* New York, NY: Random House Inc., 2007.

Mittra, Dharma. *Asanas: 608 Yoga Poses.* Novato, CA: New World Library, 2003.

Schiffman, Erich. *Yoga: The Spirit and Practice of Moving into Stillness.* New York, NY: Pocket Books, 1996.

Sparrowe, Linda. *YOGA (Yoga Journal Books).* Berkeley, CA: Hugh Levins Associates, Inc., 2002

Stephens, Mark. *Teaching Yoga: Essential Foundations and Techniques.* Berkely, CA: North Atlantic Books, 2010.

Stephens, Mark. *Yoga Adjustments: Philosophy, Principles and Techniques.* Berkeley, CA: North Atlantic Books, 2014.

Swenson, David. *Ashtanga Yoga: The Practice Manual.* Houston, TX: Ashtanga Yoga Productions, 1999.

ABOUT US

I honor you,

I am in awe of you,

I am lucky to have

you in my life,

I will never take lightly

your existence here

on this earth.

I bow in gratitude.

-Jennilee

ABOUT US

AUTHOR: JENNILEE TONER

I, Jennilee Toner, LOVE practicing and teaching yoga.

After years as a super tough Deputy Sheriff, Army Medic, Military Policewoman and Drill Sgt candidate, I found myself in 1996 practicing yoga and crying in tree pose. Those first few years I found myself in attics, basements, living rooms, garages, parks, etc. In 2000 I began to practice Bikram Yoga six days a week, both in Key West and in Massachusetts. In 2002 I added Baron Baptiste Power Yoga to the mix. In 2003 I decided I wanted to teach this wonderful form of body, mind and soul connection!

In 2008, as I completed my advanced degrees in both mythological studies and transpersonal psychology, I spent time studying Sampoorna Yoga (Sivananda lineage) with Yogi Hari at his ashram in Florida. This living master opened my mind and heart to bhakti, jnana, karma, nada and raja yoga. I have been forever changed.

In 2009 I began teaching the anatomy portion of the Frog Lotus International Teacher Training Program. Joining Vidya Jacqueline Heisel and Jennifer Yarro in training some of the best new yoga teachers this world has and will see has such a peak experience in my yoga teaching career. These two strong, beautiful and wise yoginis are AMAZING! I have learned so much from them both. I am deeply grateful to be a part of their dream!

In 2011 I created Hot Warrior Yoga, a 50plus posture sequence practiced in 90-95degrees. Hot Warrior Yoga is the BEST of both HOT HATHA and HOT VINYASA! My team and I are about to begin our seventh 200-HOUR HWY teacher training and are super excited to present, in the near future, Hot Warrior Yoga as a 27 & 54 hour advanced certification program for both yoga teachers and fitness professionals.

Also in 2011 I started teaching The Perfect Chaturanga workshops. These workshops were a call to action! Inspired by my students and their heartbreaking tales of injuries and frustrations resulting from practicing vinyasa yoga, I began to teach how to safely and intelligently practice vinyasa flow yoga. After teaching many Perfect Chaturanga workshops that first year I realized I wanted to help as many students and yoga teachers that I could. I started writing The Perfect Chaturanga book. While teaching the workshop at Wanderlust Vermont in 2013 I realized I needed help in order to turn my dream book into a reality. My talented friend, Suzanne Martin, help helped me do just that! I am so proud of this gem of an anatomy and injury prevention book you hold in your hands today!

I am such a lucky and grateful lady...everyday I find myself falling deeper and more madly in love with practicing and teaching yoga. The journey within is an ever so important one. The science and practice of yoga helps us to know ourselves, each other and the planet. Yoga quiets the diseases of the mind and the body – leaving us happy, peaceful and free. I am a firm believer that the world is a better place each time we practice our yoga! Namaste.

ARTIST: SUZANNE MARTIN

Suzanne is a visual artist and yoga instructor. She began her yogic journey in 2001, studying Buddhist art and philosophy and was later introduced to the asanas of yoga as a remedy to back pain caused by an accident. Suzanne immediately fell in love with the practice as it reminded her of her many years of modern dance and ballet. It also alleviated her physical and emotional suffering In 2011, Suzanne completed the 200 hr. Hot Warrior Yoga Teacher Training along with Yoga Across America's training. Suzanne is currently working on advancing her training in ayurveda, yoga therapy, and meditation.

I am consistently amazed at the number of positive ways that yoga has changed my life, the lives of my colleagues and my students. The Perfect Chaturanga project is so important for the yogic community as yoga is rapidly growing and spreading across the world. It is so great to know that one my life's joys is flourishing and that I am able to help spread "safe and intelligent" yoga throughout the world with my illustrations. By practicing safely we can reap all the wonderful benefits and share them with all sentient beings. Om shanti and Namaste!

OTHERS ARTISTS:

KATE GLENN Kate Glenn grew up in a nice suburb of Rochester, NY where she was encouraged by her parents and teachers to pursue a career in art. She made her way down to Baltimore to attend the Maryland Institute College of Art and graduated with a BFA in interdisciplinary sculpture with a minor in cultural studies and concentration in video.

THEA TELFORD With a combination of her imagination and inspiration taken from animals, plants, her surrounding environment, and her long time love of travel and eastern culture Thea Thelford creates playful illustrations which she turns into screen prints for fabric, paper, collage and much more. Originally from the UK, Thea's obsession with India and the East led her to become a yoga teacher. In her last visit to India Thea studied 'Thangka' A Tibetan Buddhist Art Form, which fed some of her most recent projects including designing a range of T-shirt Prints for a Yoga Clothes line. As well as taking the roll of creative Director for BE ONE OM Dome Project at Suryalila Retreat Centre, which included the undertaking of creating a 76m2 mural within the Om Dome, Thea is the personal assistant to Master Yoga Teacher Vidya Heisel and the resident yoga teacher at the centre.

OUR
GRATITUDE

Appreciation
is the purest
vibration
that exists on
the planet today.

-Abraham–Hicks

CHAPTER HEADING PHOTOS

Yoga: Orphanage by Pete McBride / National Geographic Creative
Vinyasa Yoga: Amy T Adams
Sun Salutations: Corey Woodley
The Yogic Body: Jennifer Yarro
Vinyasa Yoga Injuries: Eden Hendrick & Amanda Marsh
Injury Prevention: Jennifer Yarro & Devine Kibb
The Perfect Chaturanaga: Stephanie & Stella O'Brien
Upward Facing Dog: Tristina Kennedy & Michael Fong
Downard Facing Dog: Suzanne, Savannah May Martin, & Merrill
The Perfect Chaturanga Vinyasa Sequence: Jennilee & Baby G
Advanced Chaturanga Practice: Andrew & Trella Dolgin by Monika Broz Photography
Conclusion: Tessa Juhl, Sjonum St Cyr, Jennifer Yarro, Danielle Gismondi, Alicia Bargh
Appendix A: Language of the Asanas: Jennilee in Varanasi
Appendix B: Yogis Library: Students at FFLV
Our Gratitude: Justin and Camancha Wolfer
Our Charities: Cow at FFLV
About US: Jennilee & Suzanne

MODELS: Yogis and Yoginis

Stephanie Dufort Sherman 99-101, 178-179, 184-185
Jenny Ann Fouche p115, 124-125
Trainer Brian Baia p102
Steve Adams p133-135
Kelly Lephart p33, 33, 35, 37, 119-121, 166-167, 171, 173, 175
Aaron Styles p144-151, 185
Vicki Brignati p152-153
Jamella Anderson p156-157
Melissa Leach p158-161
Thad Smith p162-163
Wendy Akroyd p164-165
Rindha Reddy p168-169
Christina Cho p170
Amy T Adams 176-177
Lisa O'Brien 180-181

ALL 286 KICKSTARTER BACKERS...
THANK YOU!

OUR EDITORS

Jennifer Yarro: Metta Mama, thank you so much! You are my anatomy mentor, my yoga sister and a very dear for-life friend. You amaze me with your depth of knowledge about the human body, your awareness of the workings of the human mind, and your kindness, compassion and dedication to EASE and SUPPORT. I bow in love and gratitude. www.jenniferyarro.com, www.froglotusyoga.com, www.triplegemthaimassage.com

Nanda O'Leary: Our fellow Hot Warrior Yoga Goddess Nanda...we love you so! The mere thought of you makes us SO HAPPY!!! Your intellect, your humor, your beauty, love and grace... we want to know and hug you forever! Thank you for all your edits...WE NEEDED YOU!!!

SUPPORT TEAM

We could not have done this without you all! Thank you Dan and doggies for coping with a messy house, no food in the fridge, unpaid pile of bills and Jennilee's intense and passionate love affair with the computer (especially during the Kickstarter campaign!) Thank you Neal for your sacrifices while Suzanne, both pregnant and then nursing, worked endlessly on the book that no lunches EVER got made. Thank you Savannah May for putting up with so many babysitters while your Mommy worked so hard to make this happen! And THANK YOU BABYSITTERS: Myung Cha, Leslie Barkman, Willard Martin, Andie So Hum, Andie Sibincich, Jamella Anderson and Jenny Ann Fouche.

OUR
CHARITIES

May the long time Sun
Shine upon you,
All love surround you,
And the pure light
within you
Guide your way on.

-Irish Blessing

CHARITIES

Food For Life Vrindavan

It feels so right to give a percentage of this yoga book back to the motherland of yoga – India! It was in November 2013, during her trip to Varanasi, Rishikesh and Vrindavan, India, that Jennilee fell in love with all those who run, serve and participate in Food For Life Vrindavan. What began in 1990 as mission to feed sweet rice to the poor has turned into a primary and secondary school with 1300 students, a hospital that gives free medical care to about 800 villagers and students per month, a care for the cow center that hosts a herd of 250, Trees for Life project to replant and replenish, Water for Life project that helps clean the drinking water of 11 villages, a paper recycling plant, Bull Power transportation, and an organic farm. FFLV is dedicated to being, and educating other to be, GREEN! **www.fflvrindavan.org**

Mindful Yoga Therapy

For Jennilee, having served her country in the US Army, and for Suzanne, having a father, grandfather and many other family members who served in the US Marines and US Army, it was very important to give back to those that have given so much. Jennilee's good friend, colleague and fellow soldier Chris Eder is the Director of Communications at Mindful Yoga Therapy. MYT's mission is to "Help Veterans to find a calm and steady body/mind to continue productive and peaceful lives through the support of the mindful practices of yoga and education." *In 2013, our goal is to produce 10,000 Yoga for Veterans Toolkits, each of which includes a complete suite of yoga resources. We'll distribute these to military and Veteran hospital facilities, Soldier and Family Assistance Centers, and wellness programs for wounded warriors. In 2014, we plan to increase that number to 30,000, and include active duty men and women as well as Veterans.* It is our pleasure to give 5% of our profits to help **founder Suzanne Manafort, Chris and all the great folks at MYT reach their goals! www.mindfulyogatherapy.org**

Lion's Gate Sanctuary

A third charity was added right before this book went to print! Jennilee knew instantly when she heard the tales of a 550 lb. coffee drinking black bear named Cholo that she wanted to give 5% of her profits to Joan Laub, Peter Winney and their 20 lions and tigers and bears (oh my!) Lion's Gate Sanctuary was established in 2007 to provide a safe, permanent home to displaced wildlife and exotic animals born into the "system." *Unfortunately, through no fault of their own, the fate of these animals is to live out the duration of their lives in captivity. Our primary goal is to provide an environment for our residents that is conducive to a happy, tranquil life filled with love, respect and the very best of care. We believe that this is the least we can do for the amazing animals that call Lion's Gate home.* It is with great pleasure we give in order to help feed these large furry ones (5,000 lbs. of meat and 16,000 lbs. of produce a month!) and build new enclosures for their comfortable retirement. **www.lionsgatesanctuary.com**

Mind: For Better Mental Health

Jennilee's very good friend, colleague and artist extraordinaire Thea Thelford donated three beautiful pieces of art to The Perfect Chaturanga (Opening Ganesha, Closing Ganesha OM and the Shiva-Shakti on page). These three glorious pieces will be re-produced on postcards and sent out to every Kickstarter backer as a big Thank You. Also, these postcards will be for sale both on Jennilee's workshop/book tour and The Perfect Chaturanga website. All profits will go to Thea's chosen charity, London based Mind. *Our vision: We won't give up until everyone experiencing a mental health problem gets both support and respect. Our mission: We provide advice and support to empower anyone experiencing a mental health problem. We campaign to improve services, raise awareness and promote understanding. Our goals: Staying well, Empowering choice, Improving services and support, Enabling social participation, Removing inequality of opportunity, and Organisational excellence.* **www.mind.org.uk**

LOKHA SAMASTA SUKHINO BHAVANTU

May all beings be happy and free

May all beings know peace

May we do all that we can

In our thoughts words and actions

To help in this process

Cover   Mandala by Realillusion/Dreamstime
5:       Drawing by Thea Thelford
14:      Photo: Orphanage by Pete McBride/National Geographic Creative
         Grunge background, excellent texture by HorenkO/Shutterstock (also on p24,30,40,46,56, 96,116,130,142,182,186,190,198,206, 210,214)
16:      Yogic Seal, unknown Indus Valley Civilization sealmaker from Mohenjodaro archaeo logical site. Background to seal: Cracked Grey Slate by Davidschrader/Depositphotos
16-17:   Oriental flower in the middle of background. Beautiful floral oriental border in vintage style. by Nezabudkina/Shutterstock (also on p. 217)
18   Border to illustration: simple black tattoo ornamental decorative frame by 100ker/ Shutterstock; Silo of Buddha. Thailand. by Wasan Ritthawon
19:      Shiva/Shakti Drawing by Thea Thelford
21:      Hand-Drawn Abstract Henna (mehndi) Paisley Doodle Vector Illustration Design Elements by blue67design/Shutterstock (also on p 42)
22-23:   Shiv Dayal Singh: Unknown, derivative work: Saibo.
         Lahiri Mahasaya: Photo from Autobiography of a Yogi by Paramahansa Yogananda
         Swami Sivananda Saraswati: Photo of Krishnanda and Sivananda circa 1945 Unknown.
         Trumalai Krishnamacharya Drawing by Kate Glem
         Bhagawan Nityananda by Unknown taken during Nityananda's teen years..
         Swami Rama by Unkown, 19th century, around 1890-1900.
         Swami Kripalvananda by Unkown, 19th century)
         Yogi Bhajan by Unknown, 19th century
26   Sri Tirumalai Krishnamacharya and Sri Krishna Pattabhi Jois Drawings by Kate Glenn
27   Paddleboard photo courtesy of Stephanie O'Brien
         Aerial yoga photo courtesy of Lisa O'Brien
         Acro yoga photo courtesy of Jennifer Yarro
40-41   Yogic Body photo courtesy of Jennifer Yarro
42   Background pattern to Koshas Illustration: Henna Mandala Border/Yayimages
44   Organs within center figure: Illustration of male digestive system artwork by SK Chaven/Shutterstock
56   Injury Prevention photo courtesy of Jennifer Yarro
61   Prana photo courtesy of Alicia Bargh
74   Leonardo da Vinci: The Proportions of the Human Figure (Vitruvian Manek) (1490; Pen, ink and watercolour over metalpoint)
94   Inset photo: Sexy model with purple wig and intense make-up trapped in a spider web - fashion shoot by matusciac/Depositphotos
         Body Pattern: Seamless spider web. Connected white lines on black background by ihor_seamless/Shutterstock
96   The Perfect Chaturanga photo courtesy of Stephanie O'Brien
116   Upward Facing Dog photo courtesy of Tristina Kennedy
182   Photo of Andrew and Trella Dolgin courtesy of Monika Broz photography
186   Ladies in Tree photo courtesy of Jennifer Yarro
192-97   Pattern: Beautiful floral round pattern in vintage oriental style by Nezabudkina/ Shutterstock
198   Quote from Mevlana Jelalu'ddin Rumi, www.blog.gaim.com
212   Quote from Abraham-Hicks, www.abraham-hicks.com
200-05   Pattern: Vector card. Oriental flower in the middle of background. Beautiful floral oriental border in vintage style. Nezabudkina/ Shutterstock
212-13   Beautiful black and white abstract flower. With leaves and flourishes. by Jane_Hulinska
214   Our Gratitude photo courtesy of Justin and Camancha Wolfer
223   Ganesha ohm by Thea Carlson

CPSIA information can be obtained at www.ICGtesting.com
Printed in the USA
LVOW05s2043230915

455473LV00021B/188/P